THE KNIGHTS OF MALTA

JOSEPH ATTARD

BDL PUBLISHING

BDL Publishing
13, Giorgio Preca Street,
San Gwann SGN 3511, Malta.

First Edition 1992
Reprinted 1993, 1995
Revised edition 2010

ISBN: 978-99957-20-61-2

Text © Joseph Attard
Cover Design by © Book Distributors Limited
Layout and design by © Book Distributors Limited

General photography © Oliver Gatt
Artwork on pages 21, 30, 32, 37, 38, 109 © Stephen C. Spiteri
Images on pages 2, 3, 7, 12, 29, 97, 134 — Wikipedia Commons
Photography on pages 81, 99, 100, 111, 121, 131 © Maurizio Urso
Images from postcards on pages 163, 166–170 — Anthony J. Abela Medici

Back Cover
The armoury of Grand Master Alof de Wignacourt © Daniel Cilia

Printed by Gutenberg Press, Tarxien

CONTENTS

By the same author

iv

FOREWORD

Much as time and my books have confirmed that I was a born writer, I had never cast myself as a historian. Yet, my writings were always at their best when I wrote history. The more so when this concerned Malta with its many colourful periods of foreign domination.

Indeed, all my books of whatever genre contain a historical element, but the first work which brought this inclination of mine into the open was The Battle of Malta. This work, which was first published in London, had a far wider circulation all over the world than I could have expected, and it is still going strong today. Then, having written of Malta's epic when the Island was at war as a British colony, it was to be expected that I would follow up as I did with Britain and Malta – The Story of an Era which was the story of the 180 years of British occupation of Malta, especially after the Island had become an independent republic. This was another book that gave me much satisfaction.

However, during my research which is a must with every one of my books, I could not help being struck by the way in which the two above-mentioned periods of Malta's history were somehow superimposed on another similarly important period when, for 268 years, the Maltese Islands were occupied by the Order of St John of Jerusalem. If at first my interest in delving into the history of this period was primarily in tracing its relation to the others, I soon found it expanding to include the rich panorama of the Order's reign, with the roles of the various grand masters and their knights, their place in history, and the glittering epoch in which they lived. To sustain the sense of attraction that took hold of me for this story then, there was the continued public interest in the knights of Malta despite the passage of over 200 years from their time, and this is understandable in Malta where they left behind so much of the country's heritage. I was soon convinced that no matter how much writing we may have on the history of Malta, this would never be enough if due consideration is not given to the knights of Malta and their times. This was what made me write this book.

My first intention was to go into as much detail as possible, especially since we have in Malta the archives and records of the Order which have now been very efficiently catalogued. But then the language and style in which these were written would have made mine a mammoth task. Moreover, since the work I embarked upon was aimed for the general reader, I had to be restricted by length, time, and other factors. So, while I made use of the archives when required, I had resort to other sources for the material I needed for my story. These sources have been duly acknowledged in the bibliography at the end of this book, which for reasons already stated is certainly far from being a complete one. It remains for other historians to unearth more of the extensive records that exist on the knights of Malta in French, Italian, and Spanish. I wish to record my indebtedness to the above indicated sources for what information I drew for my story, as I also thank the local Association of the knights of Malta for what help it afforded me. As always I must also mention Dr Vincent Depasquale who on this occasion as well was very helpful with comments and information on the subject. I also owe a debt of thanks to my publishers who provided the illustrations and in many other ways helped to produce this publication.

Joseph Attard

1

IN PALESTINE, CYPRUS, AND RHODES

The land of Palestine where Jesus Christ lived, died, and arose from death, has never ceased to be considered as the Holy Land. For centuries afterwards, it had become the pious practice for men and women from Europe and the West to make pilgrimages to the Lord's Sepulchre and the other Holy Places. Even when Jerusalem first fell into Muslim hands in the seventh century, notwithstanding the difficulties that were then arising, mostly because of sentiments of individual rulers, such pilgrimages continued to be allowed. Charlemagne, one of the foremost Holy Roman Emperors, opened hospices in Jerusalem for the accommodation of such pilgrims.

But, with the approach of the eleventh century and the advent of new Muslim rulers, the position changed. There began the harassing and ill-treatment of pilgrims, which was climaxed by the Fatimite Caliph Hakim, a fanatical and demented tyrant who in 1009 razed the Holy Sepulchre to the ground and destroyed all Christian property.

Thirty years after Hakim's death, a number of charitable merchants from Amalfi (in Italy) rebuilt the hospices and the church of the Holy Sepulchre. But this did not remove the difficulties that continued to face pilgrims and Christians

The sixteenth century city walls of Jerusalem, built by Sultan Suleiman the Magnificent

in Palestine. It was a situation which raised much ferment in Europe and, instigated by the fiery sermons of an English preacher, Peter the Hermit, and Pope Urbanus II, many of Europe's adventurous princes were enticed to embark on a Crusade to regain the Holy Places from the Saracens. As soon as the pope launched a Holy Crusade against the Ottomans, a number of groups of disorganized knights and common people followed leaders who preached that, with God's help, they would defeat the enemy. These were the Peoples' Crusades. Yet, the first official Crusade was led by European princes and was to be successful.

This successful turn of events encouraged the Amalfitan congregation by now engaged as hospitallers in a Benedictine hospital dedicated to St John the Baptist in Jerusalem to rally round their leader Blessed Gerard. He was a patrician of Scala and a Benedictine, who was now all out to expand the congregation into an Order of St John of Jerusalem. Grateful lords and princes who had been healed of their wounds in the hospital were soon bestowing portions of their estates on the newly founded Order enabling it not only to stand on its feet but also to establish its future 'commanderies' and daughter homes in various places of Europe. In 1113 Pope Paschal II took the

Blessed Gerard, founder of the Order of the Knights Hospitallers

Order under his protection and gave Brother Gerard a new and more militant constitution in gratitude for services rendered. The original document recording this important point in the history of the Order can still be found in the Malta Library. It reads that 'Pope Paschal II grants to his venerable son, Gerard, founder and provost of the Hospital in Jerusalem, a charter of incorporation of the Order of the Hospital of St John of Jerusalem beyond or on this side of the sea, that is to say, in Asia or in Europe', thus placing it as an exempt Order of the Church under the direct protection of the Apostolic See.

With the resumption of fighting with the Saracens, some of the knights of the Order had to become soldiers, and with new readily found recruits to the cause, there was formed the element of knights of the Temple or Templars. Even this Order soon gained much power and importance since its members were required to do the actual fighting with the Muslim infidels. The many remarkable forts and castles built by the Templars in the course of their fighting years still crown strategic heights in Palestine, Syria, and Jordan.

Nonetheless, another Crusade in 1147 was a complete failure and it was only in 1180 that enough elements could be rallied for another. When this set forth it included amongst the leaders King Richard I of England who was largely responsible for what successes were obtained, and was soon being known as Coeur de Lion, the Lion-heart. However, more than by the lassitude that was now creeping in, the Order was plagued by quarrels between the leaders. The element of chivalry which had become the epitome of the Crusades began to be tarnished, and it was not long before King Richard was left to fight his battles alone. It was by his implacable certainty and singleness of purpose, as well as by his overwhelming energy and self-sacrifice, that he managed to win the battle for Acre. But that was the end, for he realized soon after that alone as he was, his had become a lost cause. So he left Palestine and his departure might have marked the end of the Crusades.

With the Templars in Cyprus in 1191, it befell to the other knights who had until then been more of a nursing brotherhood to take up arms when required to defend pilgrims in the Holy Land. This further emphasized the military role to the Order, which continued to grow in strength, influence, and possessions. It was now that the Order acquired the additional character of an Order of Knighthood, with its member knights being bound by the three monastic vows of chastity, obedience, and poverty. Even so, with their next spurt of activity in 1291, the Muslims occupied the last Christian strongholds, and with its position in Palestine becoming untenable, the Order moved to Cyprus. This was only Hobson's choice since the island did not provide the right environment for the scheme of reorganization and perfection there was intended for the Order. Moreover, there was the unpleasant realization that, since their transfer to Cyprus a hundred years before, the Templars had succumbed to the temptations of power and were believed to have been drawn towards Freemasonry and other secret intrigues which certainly clashed with the ideals of the Order. And this brought even stronger pressure on the knights to find a new home.

It took them 19 years to do this, and in 1307 the knights started the attack on Rhodes. Although by early September they were already in possession of the greater part of the island, they had to wait for another two years before all the island was brought under their control. The pope had also confirmed their possession of the island and its immediate territory. A

The Siege of Acre, 1291

year after the knights of St John had moved there, in 1309, the Templars had sunk so deep in their intrigues that their institution was suppressed. Five years later in 1314, their last Grand Master Jacques de Molay, was burned at the stake in Paris. The Hospitallers inherited a good part of their property. But there was the more important fact that the Order of St John was left with a clear field to attract the

Historic castle and harbour in Kyrenia

noble youth of Europe's aristocracy, and to go ahead with the reorganization it badly wanted to carry out.

Besides being one of the most beautiful islands in the Mediterranean, Rhodes was very fertile and fruitful. Another important factor was its geological structure which provided ample strong rock and sites for the knights to build their fortifications. With this point settled, the grand master at the time, Foulques de Villaret who was one of the Order's best, could carry on with the reorganization so that the Order could evolve its characteristic form based on the same old vows of chastity, obedience, and poverty.

The knights were divided into five groups. Firstly there were the military knights of justice who in a sense dominated the Order. These were all to be of noble birth from both parents for at least four generations, and in fact it can be said that all military knights were the sons of the greatest families in Europe. All requests to join the Order began to be carefully scrutinized and no exceptions were made. Applicants that were accepted were conferred with the accolade of knighthood with some pomp. Accompanied by the grand cross, who would have just dubbed them, they would walk bareheaded in the armour and robes worn at the investiture. Their comrades would receive them in the hall of the auberge where they would be made to sit on a carpet laid on the ground, and be offered bread, salt, and a glass of water. The knight presiding at the ceremony, however, would later on that day give a banquet to the new knights and his friends, as if to make up for the sense of austerity conveyed by the ceremonial. The new aspirant knights had then to undergo a novitiate of one year before they could join the Convent (as the central body of the Order was called) for military service, and with each year of such duty being termed a *caravan*. Then, after three such caravans, a knight would have to reside for at least two years in the Convent. After completing duties with the Order, the knights were free to return to their home in Europe, but they would always be subject to recall by the grand master in case of need. Promotions to the higher posts of bailiff, commander, or prior were made from this group.

The second group in the Order was reserved for ecclesiastical service as chaplains or chaplains of obedience. The incumbents who would receive holy orders were normally expected to work in hospitals or the churches of the convent, but were still not exempted from duties in the caravans. They were eligible for promotion to priors and even bishops of the Order. The third group, the serving brothers, were only required to be respectable and not necessarily of noble birth. These were required to do military service. The fourth and fifth groups were the honorary knights in the grades of magisterial knights and knights of grace as nominated by the grand master.

There was a further division made on the basis of nationality with the knights being placed under one of eight langues (tongues). These were those of Aragon, Auvergne, Castile, England (with Scotland and Ireland), France, Germany, Italy, and Provence. Having three French langues was not incidental since the French had a numerical preponderance in the Order.

Command was vested in a grand master who was elected by his brother knights on the basis of years of efficient services in the major positions. The grand master was also the president of the supreme council (Sacro Consiglio) which included also the bishop, priors, conventual bailiffs, knights grand cross, and deans of the langues. As for what one could call general administration procedures, there was the chapter general to be normally convened every five years, sometimes even after ten. However, meetings were announced a year ahead so as to give chance to the various langues and individual knights to submit drafts for reforms. The symbol of the Order continued to be the eight-pointed cross introduced by Grand Master Raymond du Puy, representing the eight beatitudes, with the four arms being also symbolical of the four virtues of Prudence, Temperance, Fortitude, and Justice. The vows taken by the knights were proof of the religious character of the Order. Newly proposed members embraced and kissed each other in token of friendship, peace, and brotherly love; hence they called each other frater.

With the taking of Rhodes from the Byzantines and the eventual rule over the island, there commenced the recognition of the distinct sovereignty of the Order. Thus all Christian Powers and Catholic nations began to look at the Order in its full descriptive title of the Sovereign Military Order of St John of Jerusalem. With its grand master also styled prince of Rhodes, it continued to grow into a more powerful and wealthy body of celibate nobles vowed to carry out the tasks of tending the poor, healing the sick, and waging a perpetual war on Islam in the Mediterranean. This last vow could not perhaps be rigidly adhered to since with Rhodes being an island, the knights could not very well pursue military action on land. Nonetheless they had still to provide and maintain their weapons which included a coat of mail and plate armour both for the knight and his horse. Each had to have three horses (a battle-charger, a palfrey or courser, and a pack-horse). They had also to have and pay attendants to carry their shields and their banner. However, they were soon building more galleys and other ships which made it possible for them to mount more attacks on enemy shipping crossing from and to nearby Turkey. Indeed it was not long before the knights added seamanship to their other attributes even to the extent of being eventually considered to have become Christian corsairs.

Although the spirit of the Crusades had long been dead and Christian states were often on friendly terms with Moslem and Mongol conquerors, the Order never lost sight of the danger which still threatened Christendom and persisted with its vow to fight Islam with or without assistance of others. The earliest naval action on record by the knights from Rhodes concerned the grand master himself, Foulques de Villaret, who had previously been one of the Order's admirals, who with a small force destroyed 23 Turkish coastal vessels in 1312. He was soon being emulated by the Grand Commander Albert of Schwarzbourg who, supported by Genoese corsairs, led a mixed fleet of 24 galleys and defeated 50 Ottomans at Ephesus. Hardly had a year passed by when Schwarzbourg with eight vessels of the Order and six Genoese galleys routed a fleet of 80 Turkish vessels.

In 1334 the Alliance of Avignon was signed whereby the king of France, Venice, the papal navy, and the king of Cyprus rallied under the standard of the Order in an attempt to fan the embers of the Crusades. Together they destroyed an Ottoman fleet in a naval battle in the Gulf of Smyrna in Turkey and then proceeded to capture the town. It seems that the fourteenth century was characterized by every Christian nation wanting to have a fling at the Muslims as long as there was the Order to lead them or contribute ships for the action. The Order was always ready to oblige, as if it considered its mission as being touched by divine approval and, with the meek arrogance of the religious, it might have even viewed opposition to its will as akin to apostasy. In an unpublished manuscript of 'A Knight of St John', Averil Mackenzie-Grieve had this to say about those times, 'The galleys of St John were famous throughout Europe. In them the knights made the swift, dauntless attacks. Their exploits were published in broadsheets in Naples, in Marseilles, and in Venice. They became almost mythical. But strong men were needed for the galleys. These were overcrowded with slave oarsmen, fighting men, and crew, cumbered with arms and provisions, so that often it was impossible to lie down to sleep. There was neither shade from the blazing sun nor shelter from rain and sea-water. Swept by sudden storms, the food would become sodden and useless, the men sick or fever struck. After a successful encounter, the galleys would be still more overcrowded with captives and booty.' The Order's exploits in those times still elicit admiration when considering its limitations in size and strength in confronting mighty Islam. One wonders how, in 1347, the Prince of Catalonia Fra Arnaldo de Peres Tortes managed to burn 100 Turkish craft at Imbros. Ten years later the combined fleets of the Order and Venice under Raymond Berengar destroyed 35 Muslim ships. In 1361 Ferlino d'Airasca, one of the Order's admirals, at the head of his own squadron and helped by Christian corsairs, captured Adalia (Satalia) but his greatest exploit came in 1365 when he sacked Alexandria with only 16 galleys.

Not all the Order's naval actions were strictly of a military nature. There were occasions when the knights played the part of Christian corsairs as they had indeed been dubbed. On the many occasions in which they seized Muslim ships, they would return to their nests laden with plunder of spices, silks, gold, and jewels. The loot went to the Order's coffers, while the men were taken as slaves for their galleys. In 1393 and again in 1399, the Order's galleys penetrated into the Black Sea and attacked the hornets' nests of corsairs long established there. In the first instance they did not do too well since they lost Grand Master de Heredia who fell into the hands of the enemy with many other knights. But they made up on the second occasion. Such were the risks of the game they were playing.

It was, however, no game at all. The sallies made by the Order's ships did a lot of damage to Islamic shipping, but most of all to its pride. Something had to be done and, indeed throughout the fifteenth century, enemy pressure on Rhodes continued to rise.

The beginning of this turn of events came at Castelrosso, an outpost of the knights which fell to the Mamelukes of Egypt in 1440. Nineteen enemy ships also invaded Rhodes itself, but the knights under Grand Master Lastic repulsed the attack and followed the Muslims right to Anatolia where they pursued the enemy ashore killing 700 men at the cost of 60 knights. In 1444, there was another unsuccessful attempt to invade Rhodes. At this time, however, there was a growing risk poised by the Ottoman Turks under Muhammad Fatih 'the Conqueror' who swore an oath to launch a determined attack upon Christendom.

He first captured Costantinople in 1453, followed by the islands of Cos, Lemnos, and Lesbos in the Dodecanese group four years later.

Suleiman the Magnificent
Sultan of the Ottoman Empire

These Muslim successes were certainly no flashes in the pan and the knights realized how these could well be tactical moves to surround Rhodes by potential outposts to attack their island headquarters. In 1462 the Order's chapter general met specifically to consider the situation. It was decided that, considering that Rhodes was already well fortified, as indeed it was and with such fortifications that can be seen even today, a special effort had to be made to bring the fleet to the highest levels of efficiency and preparation. Two years later there was something else to worry the knights: the pope tried to raise a combined fleet against the Muslims but, because of internal dissension, all the Christian states stayed back. It seemed clear to the Order that henceforth it would have to face Islam alone.

There was a few years' respite after 1481 when Muhammad Fateh died and his sons began fighting each other. Grand Master d'Aubusson was wise enough to use this time to increase the efficiency of the Order's forces as it had been decided. As proof of the success of this measure, Admiral Ludovicus di Scalenghe captured a number of Turkish ships in 1502. As if to allay any remaining doubts and fears, five years later the Order achieved its biggest victory after a sanguinary battle with a combined Muslim fleet off Alexandretta. But the knights could not have known this was to be their last victory, and the beginning of the end of their stay in Rhodes of more than two centuries!

Suleiman the Magnificent, the great-grandson of Muhammad Fateh, now the powerful sultan of the Ottomans, had not for one moment forgotten the Order of St John. He had always admired its growing prowess and, since acceding to the throne, he had cultivated further a sense of chivalrous respect for the knights and their new Grand Master Philippe Villiers de L'Isle-Adam. Nonetheless, these feelings were still outweighed by his determination to honour the oath of his forefathers and to throw the Order out of Rhodes. He bided his time until he could rally every vessel, every man, and every engine of war under the flag of Islam. Then, in 1522, he launched his attack on Rhodes.

Although the Order's fleet was in a state of preparedness, it was hopelessly outnumbered. So, rather than wasting his vessels, L'Isle-Adam disembarked his knights to strengthen his garrison on the island. But Suleiman persisted with his pressure and besieged the defenders of Rhodes. After six months of siege, and betrayal by one of their own, d'Amaral, the decimated and half-starved knights were forced to capitulate on Christmas Eve of that same year. Their heroic stand fired even further Suleiman's admiration and Grand Master L'Isle-Adam together with his remaining knights were not only allowed to leave Rhodes unmolested, but were also given a ceremonial guard of honour to see them off the island in their own galleys.

The Order was defeated, but not dishonoured. It retained its high prestige, and although in a state of disorder, it was given the chance to recoup and fight another day. Its only immediate problem was again in finding a new home.

St Catherine's Gate, the main entrance to the town of Rhodes

2

THE KNIGHTS IN MALTA

Emperor Charles V of Spain wore the crown of the Holy Roman empire. He had however also brought under his rule the dynasties of Castile, Aragon, and Burgundy, as well as the Austrian possessions of the House of Habsburg, the Netherlands, Luxembourg, Sardinia, Sicily, the greater part of Italy and Spanish conquests in North Africa and the New World. Now he allowed the Order of St John to use Sicily as a *pied à terre* until it could find a new home.

The knights rallied to the banner of L'Isle-Adam in his temporary Convent at Syracuse. With them they carried all they could take out of Rhodes, including the galleys many of which were the knights' own individual private property. Both the Order and the individual owner knights used to have their large vessels built in various European shipyards, and it so happened that on 1 January, 1523 when they evacuated Rhodes, there was launched at Nice the carrack *St Anne* which had been constructed for the Order. This was eventually to be consigned to the knights at Syracuse and join the remnants of their fleet there. But it would not be amiss to say something more about this carrack since besides epoch making she had to play more important parts in the history of the Order.

Carracks were heavy ships used for the carrying of stores and troops as well as anything else that could not be carried in galleys or smaller boats. They were not as mobile as the lighter vessels and of course not so swift. But then they were more heavily armed and this made them valuable as auxiliaries to any fleet. The *St Anne* was 132 feet long and 40 feet in the beam. Her super-structure rose 75 feet above the waterline. She could carry 4,000 tons of stores or merchandise, and had stowage for six months' victuals. Moreover, she had a blacksmith's, shop, a bakery, luxurious saloons

The Grand Carrack Sant' Anna

and cabins, as well as a chapel. Her armament consisted of fifty long range guns and a number of falconets and demi-cannon while her armoury held personal weapons for five hundred men. She had a crew of 300, but could also carry an additional 400 light infantry or cavalry. However, the most important feature in the *St Anne* was that it was sheathed in metal and was cannon proof. She was therefore the first ever armoured war vessel to be built and adapted to resist the projectiles of her own time. The Order had three other carracks, the *Santa Caterina*, *San Giovanni* and the *Santa Maria* which was captured from the Muslims.

It immediately became obvious that the knights could not all be accommodated at the Convent of Syracuse so some of them began to be given other temporary homes. After the loss of Rhodes, and their subsequent arrival in Europe, the Order stopped for different periods in various cities, namely Candia (modern Crete), Syracuse, Messina, Civitavecchia, Nice, and finally settled in Viterbo. The periodical council meetings began to be held in Syracuse aboard the new carrack *St Anne*. It was to be expected that the subject most frequently discussed at such meetings would be the finding of a new home for the Order. But Grand Master L'Isle-Adam was not in agreement. Rather than looking for a new place, he preferred to seek assistance to mount an attack and recapture Rhodes. It was with this aim in view that he set out from Syracuse to wander from one Court to another in Europe begging for help. Because of the preponderance of French knights in the Order he went first to the King of France with his proposal, but Francis I was more concerned trying to obtain help from Suleiman against his enemy Emperor Charles V of Spain. Wherever L'Isle-Adam went after this there was more or less always the same negative reply. It appeared as if however respected the Order might have been for its fighting prowess, it was no longer popular. This could have been because of the knights' direct allegiance to the Pope and their vow to fight only the Infidel which therefore made them insusceptible and useless for national allegiances. The more so when at the time nationalism was becoming the dominant force in European affairs. One cannot of course rule out the possibility that because of its riches and influence the Order might have become suspect. On the other hand one cannot rule out the fear and apprehension that had crept in amongst European nations of Suleiman the Magnificent who in the course of his sultanate had not only conquered nations in the Persian Gulf and the shores of the Arabian Sea, but had also reached Belgrade and Budapest in Europe with his armies and added them to his Ottoman empire which was then at the peak of its glory.

It was only when L'Isle-Adam went to King Henry VIII of England that he received a somewhat different reply. He didn't expect anything different from the others, and if anything he was prepared for the worst since the English monarch had by then already begun his quarrelling with the Pope about his marital affairs, and was seeing the Order in England in a bad light. Yet he received L'Isle-Adam with much respect at St James Palace and finished by giving him guns and armour to the value of 20,000 crowns. Much as these were appreciated they could be of very little help to the project. What the grand master wanted most was the support of galleys and troops. After the 19 guns given by the English monarch were taken to Malta via Syracuse by the Knight Sir John Sutton in January, 1530 they were eventually sent to be used in the defence of Tripoli. It was only recently that one of them was dug out from the bottom of Famagusta Harbour. It was identified by the badge of the Tudors it had on it, as well as the coat of arms of L'Isle-Adam.

L'Isle-Adam returned to Sicily a very disappointed man. He knew he would have to drop his plan for an attack on Rhodes, as he very well knew, that spread out as they were and away from his watchful eyes the knights were now going to be more susceptible to be touched by worldly aspirations and relax their monastic vows. There was also the question of idleness which could easily turn their formation into decay. This led him to the conclusion that unless a new home was found soon, the Order would very likely disintegrate.

Emperor Charles V was asked about the possibility of giving the Maltese Islands to the homeless Order. The situation was difficult for the Order as they felt the necessity to have their own headquarters in order to continue with their fight against the Ottomans. The Emperor was inclined to agree. After all he knew those islands were mere barren rocks without vegetation and with scanty soil and water, and he had never made any use of them. But being the person he was he wanted something in return. He did not have money in mind, but something that would take off some heavy burden from his shoulders. Malta had already been a regular target for raids by corsairs which made her more of a useless possession. But what was causing him a bigger headache was Tripoli and he was very much stretched to maintain this dependency as a Christian enclave lost as it was amongst the Barbary States of North Africa. Why not hand it to the knights to defend, and this as a condition to the transfer of Malta? The idea appealed to him and the offer was made to the Order.

L'Isle-Adam was not taken in by the offer. He immediately realized where the snag was. But he could not refuse the offer outright. Time was running out fast and even his stay in Sicily was only being tolerated at the pleasure of the Emperor. The least he could do was to ask for time until he could have a report made out about Malta. But when he received this from a commission he had quickly sent to the island, he was even more perturbed.

The island of Malta, the report said, was a rock of soft sandstone about seven leagues long and three or four wide. Its surface was barely covered with three or four feet of earth, mostly stony and unfit for cultivation. Where this was possible the Maltese grew cotton and cumin which they exchanged for grain, as they also cultivated some fruit. With the exception of a few springs there was no running water, and the 12,000 inhabitants of Malta, and another 5,000 in the sister island of Gozo were largely poor farmers living in primitive villages. There was only one town which was the capital. In the way of defence then there were only two castles where the inhabitants took shelter during raids by corsairs. It was a dismal picture that was given, which only brightened a little when the report mentioned that the island of Malta had two spacious harbours capable of housing many galleys.

With the Order having become a powerful maritime power harbours would be useful and L'Isle-Adam couldn't do without them anywhere he might have gone since the Order's coffers had always been filled to necessity by clean piracy. This needed ships, and these in turn needed harbours. And that was the only positive point that he registered in his deliberations. Nonetheless, under normal circumstances L'Isle-

Grand Master L'Isle-Adam landing in Malta — 26 October 1530

Adam would not have accepted the Emperor's gift, but at the time there were other things pressing on his tired mind. One and which was not the least amongst them was that some of the knights, tired of waiting were already leaving the Convent to return to their by now impoverished commanderies in Europe, and this might have flashed the first sign of the disintegration of the Order he feared. Indeed the situation had become one where beggars could not be the choosers. So L'Isle-Adam accepted the offer.

The document in the form of a receipt by Charles V, still preserved in the National

Malta Library, was dispatched to L'Isle-Adam, 'bestowing on the knights in order that they may perform in peace the duties of their Religion for the benefit of the Christian community and employ their forces and arms against the perfidious enemies of Holy Faith – the islands of Malta, Gozo and Comino in return for the yearly presentation, on All Saints Day, of a falcon to Charles, viceroy of Sicily.' And this was all conditioned, although not specifically mentioned, by the left-hand gift of Tripoli.

When the Maltese learned of this they were justifiably indignant as it was known how in 1428 King Alfonso V of Aragon had confirmed their ancient privileges and paid 30,000 gold florins which was the sum for which the impecunious monarch had pawned the islands to Don Gonsalvo Monroy, and how on that day he had sworn on the four Gospels that they (the Maltese Islands) would never be transferred to another sovereignty. Ironically enough this Magna Carta of Maltese liberties is also still to this day preserved at the National Malta Library quite close to the other document by Charles V already mentioned. However the least the Maltese could do was to send an embassy of protest to the viceroy of Sicily. But when the Maltese envoys arrived there, the galleys of the Order of St John were already in Syracuse, and Grand Master L'Isle-Adam had already been invested with the sovereignty of Malta through his representative, the bailiff of Monasca.

On 26 October 1530, Grand Master L'Isle-Adam and his knights sailed into Grand Harbour at Malta on the carrack *St Anne* to take possession of their new home.

✠   ✠   ✠

It is a fact that the majority of the people of Malta at that time had gone through hard times. Their life had been one of continuous routine of backbreaking toil to make a living, with only the occasional interruption by attacks of the Muslim corsairs who would always take slaves. And in truth these people were past caring who would rule their country. But there was also the minority which included many noble families who had grown up as freemen and were quick to assume that the coming of the knights could mean the loss of their political rights. So they began immediately to view them with suspicion. It could have also been that such Maltese attitude was also sparked by what had been described by a Maltese historian as the haughty bearing of the knights on arrival at Malta. It must be mentioned as well that rather than as one would have expected the knights to arrive covered with the laurels of their many fine achievements, the word was soon going round of how many of them had by then lost their celibate and religious vows and were also inclined towards Freemasonry as had happened in the case of the Templars. This assumption or misconception particularly shocked the members of the clergy who in their own way were already apprehensive of new rulers who were under the immediate protection of the Holy See as were the knights.

Besides their personal arms and belongings the knights did not take much with them to Malta. They certainly took their sacred icon containing one of the hands of St John the Baptist, a silver processional cross (still to be seen at the cathedral of Mdina) and some ecclesiastic vestments and treasures. The most important thing which they could not afford to leave behind, and which they carried with them was the set of

The medieval walled capital, Mdina

their archives, which today is still preserved in Malta. This makes it obvious that it was their idea to start from scratch. And so they did.

For over 200 years the Maltese had regulated their internal affairs by means of an autonomous Commune also called Università made up of four executive members styled Giurati (Jurats) presided over by an official called the captain of the Rod (della Verga). He was so called because of the rod or staff of office which was always carried behind him by a page, but was also known by the Arabic title of Hakem. Although elective and aristocratic this office was practically hereditary in the few Maltese noble families. This body of men or parliament, as it could be called, ensured Maltese liberties, and the least the Maltese were hoping for was that these arrangements would not be stopped or changed.

Grand Master L'Isle-Adam took formal possession of Malta at Mdina, a medieval town which was the island's capital.

The investure ceremonial was observed with all the pomp and formalities in which the important elements of Maltese society also participated. But the climax was reached when L'Isle-Adam proceeded to the gate of the city beneath a baldachin borne by the Giurati, and then swore upon the great cross of the cathedral and the cross of the Order of St John to observe the privileges and usages of the island as granted by the King of Aragon and Sicily. After this the captain of the Rod knelt to kiss his hand and surrender the silver keys. It was then that the gate of the city was opened to allow the grand master to enter amidst salutes and the ringing of bells.

Mdina was then Malta's only town. Its name being the Arabic meaning for a walled town. But in 1428 after the Maltese had complained to their ruler King Alfonso V of Aragon and Sicily against the pawning of the island to his nobles when he was short of cash, the King had accepted their complaint and confirmed their ancient privileges. On that occasion he had referred to Mdina as 'a notable and distinguished jewel of the royal crown.' And the Maltese then began to refer to the town in official documents as Notabile, although it remained Mdina in common parlance.

One would have expected the knights to make this which was the only town in Malta their headquarters. But instead, they preferred to establish themselves in Birgu, a small village just in the entrance of what is now Grand Harbour, and lying in the shadow of Fort St Angelo. They probably made this choice because of their seafaring service, and at Birgu they could have their galleys at hand for whatever contingency that could crop up. But even so, the village of Birgu lacked the necessary amenities and accommodation to house them, which apparently did not affect them and they began immediately to attend to these needs. In the narrow streets of the village they began to build their Auberges, one for each Langue. Where more convenient, they leased premises for this purpose, as they had done in Rhodes. They also set forth to construct bastions to surround the place and fortify it against any eventual attack. Birgu was already endowed with a magnificent church dedicated to St Lawrence which was first elected in 1090 at the time of Count Roger the Norman and embellished throughout the years. The knights now turned it into their Conventual Church.

L'Isle-Adam, also conscious of the need of defensive fortifications began work to enlarge the defences of Fort St Angelo. This stronghold which dominated Grand Harbour as it still does now, had served its purpose during the times of Carthaginians, Romans, Byzantines, Normans Angevines and Aragonese. It seems that the grand master could then perceive its eventual important use for the Order, and he started by establishing himself in the fort. He found a ready house there, built about a century before for the De Nava family then governors of St Angelo. These had also built a chapel at the same time dedicated to the 'Mother of God'. The grand master now enlarged this and rededicated it to *St Anne*. There was also work started on the walls of the town of Mdina with the same intentions of defence, and this was retained as the capital of the island.

It was a good beginning, no doubt watched and commented upon by the many islanders who were still not sure how the Order would fare in Malta. But after some time there was the expected beginning of a thaw and change. The first coinage of the Order was struck with the principal coins being the scudo, the tari, the carlino and the grano or grain. With none knowing how these denominations were to persist in Malta's coinage five centuries later. But what might have helped to bring the knights and Maltese closer was the Candlemas ceremony that was introduced. On this annual occasion, falling on 2 February when the Church celebrates the Feast of the Purification of the Blessed Virgin, the Parish Priests of Malta and Gozo began to be asked to meet the grand master, and offer him a decorated wax candle. He would then address the assembly on the problems of the day, stressing the ways and means of how state and Church could cooperate for the benefit of the people. This function was to survive right to these very days. The construction works embarked upon created work for the Maltese, while each Langue now began to bring in its men-at-arms, serving brothers, clerics, artificers, sea-captains, seamen and military engineers. These newcomers to the island scene mingled with the people with the obvious results which introduced a new way of life to the islanders.

L'Isle-Adam should have been happy since the transfer of the Order to Malta seemed to have been clicking successfully. But he wasn't. It seems that notwithstanding the faultless changeover he had still not effaced the memories of Rhodes and might have still been hoping he would one day recapture his former home. Had this been the case then his hopes might have been strengthened when his galleys had the first opportunity to strike at the Muslims from Malta, and took it. Five galleys of the Order under Admiral Bernardo Salviati, with two other Genoese vessels swooped on a Turkish fleet at Modon and destroyed it. Then they also sacked the city and returned to Malta with the loot and 800 Turkish slaves. Soon after, Salviati joined the great Genoese Admiral Andrea Doria in an attack on Coron.

These two naval actions should have lifted the spirits of L'Isle-Adam since they signified the revival of the prowess of the Order which was so essential for its future in Malta. This might have appeared to be the case when he began to refurbish his quarters in Fort St Angelo, but what interest the old grand master tried to show was only skin deep, because by now he was having troubles of a different nature. Following his debacle with the Pope, King Henry VIII of England had in 1532 declared himself Supreme Head of an English Church and began to raise difficulties to the further existence of the English branch of the Order. This was immediately reflected in Malta by the number of young nobles who began to be sent by the grand prior in England to join the Order in Malta. Members of the Langue of England had to have been born within the territorial limits assigned to their priories and commanderies in England, Ireland and Scotland, as they had also to be of noble birth. It seems however that some of the first English arrivals in Malta at this time could not readily produce documented proof of this. L'Isle-Adam gave them the benefit of the doubt and conditioned their joining the Order to the procurement of documented proof of their nobility within six months. As for aspirants and newcomers however the general assembly or chapter of the knights enforced the immediate production of such proof. Also laying down that those failing to produce it, would be sent back, with all travelling expenses having to be paid by the grand prior himself.

However what harassed L'Isle-Adam most was the insubordination of some of being schooled in the strict observance of the Order's rules were inclined to be out of hand. Some of them might have also exceeded in their follies of libertinism. And this seems to be confirmed by the addition of a disciplinary clause which the chapter of the Order added to its statute. The clause read that 'whosoever shall enter into the house of a citizen without being invited, and against the wish of the head of the family, or shall disturb the social gathering of the people during their festivals, dances, weddings or similar occasions, shall lose two years seniority without hope of pardon. Moreover, whosoever shall by day or night damage the doors and windows of the people, shall in addition suffer such rigid imprisonment as may be decreed by the grand master and Council.' It had by now become difficult if not impossible to prevent duels amongst the hot-headed youths, especially the young novices, keenly

A present day view of Fort St Angelo

alive to an affront, and ever ready to resent it. They regarded personal courage as the first of all human virtues.

There might have been some reprieve when besides aspirants for the Order there began to arrive in Malta fully fledged lords and knights like Sir Nicholas Upton, Sir Philip Babington, Sir Henry Gerard, Sir Dunstan Newdgate, Sir David Gausson, Sir Nicholas Lambert and Sir Anthony Russell, just to mention a few. These brought colour and strength to the Order, but they also brought more of the inevitable sense of pique in the English Langue.

Even with their lineage and high sense of snobbery such knights were often causing trouble. It is recorded in the Order's archives how on 13 March 1534 knights Oswald Massingberd and James Hussey came to blows with knights William Tyrrel and Nicholas Upton. The grand master and Council placed all four of them under house arrest until their case could be investigated. When it transpired that Massingberd had indeed conspired against the life of the grand master he was first imprisoned in Gozo and then condemned to the loss of the habit. But when he came to be stripped in front of the Assembly of knights gathered at the Conventual Church of St Lawrence in Birgu, Massingberd asked for mercy, and his sentence was changed to the forfeiture of the commandery he held, and two years' loss of seniority.

This kind of behaviour of the knights affected L'Isle-Adam considerably, and the frail and tired grand master died on 21 August 1534.

He was succeeded by an Italian, Pietro del Ponte who however died barely a year later in 1535. The same happened with the next grand master, the French Didier de

Saint-Jaille, who died in 1536. Neither of these had the time to come to grips with the first years of the Order in Malta.

The next grand master was Juan de Homedes who was a Spaniard. He was one of the traditional knights who like L'Isle-Adam could not at first reconcile himself with the Order's departure from Rhodes, but was then wise enough to accept it and resign himself to the fact that the Order's destiny was bound to Malta. Like L'Isle-Adam too he was a strict disciplinarian, but unlike him he did not let any incorrect behaviour by the knights to go to his head. He administered punishment where this was indicated, and left it at that. After all, punishment in the Order was not so light. When Knight Oswald Massingberd came to blows with Knight John Babington during an Assembly at the Auberge, with both of them tearing one another's beard, Massingberd got three months imprisonment in Fort St Angelo, while Babington was sentenced to quarantine which meant being placed on a low diet for 40 days, with flagellation being inflicted twice a week during this period. Even minor offences were punished, generally with what was called septaine. This meant that the knight to be punished would remain in his room and fast for seven days, with the only food to be taken on Wednesday and Friday being bread and water, while he would receive also corporal punishment during which he would be required to recite the psalm *Deus misereatur nostri*.

Juan de Homedes laid more stress on the maritime power of the Order. He strongly believed that since the Rhodes debacle Christendom had come to depend on the great maritime republics like Venice, Genoa and Amalfi, and that it was about time that the Order regained its place with them. It used to warm the cockles of his heart when from his chambers in Fort St Angelo he often watched the increasing number of galleys in harbour with the red striped sails bearing the device of their owners when they belonged to individual knights, or when common property the eight pointed cross symbol. And many a time his thoughts dwelt on what the Muslims could do to prevent the Order from regaining her place on the high seas.

The galley had always been the chief arm of the Order's Navy. This was a ship six times as long as its beam with 'lateen' sails and great oars or sweeps. The galley was normally armed with a ram. It was a beautiful ship to behold, with its heraldic finery and the many pennons, but all this concealed the hell of slavery for the oarsmen and the many discomforts of the ship's company because of overcrowding, lack of shelter from sun and rain as well as the occasional sodden food, contaminated water and bouts of fever and scurvy for knight and slave alike. It is true that in most cases oarsmen of the galleys were slaves or schiavi as they were called who were always Muslims with only some occasional Christian convicted of piracy and fortunate to escape the gallows. But there were also two other categories i.e. the Forzati who were pressed men recruited in the way of a press-gang, and the Buonevoglie who were volunteers offering their paid services for a term of years. The worst treated of the lot were the slaves and their ghastly existence in the galleys is described in the following extract from Sea Wolves of the Mediterranean by Commander E. Hamilton Currey.

They were chained six to a bench; the benches are four feet wide covered with sacking stuffed with wool, over which are thrown sheepskins which reach to the floor. The officer who is master of the galley-slaves remains aft with the captain to receive his orders; there are two under-officers, one amidships and one at the prow; all of these are armed with whips, with which they flog the absolutely naked bodies of the slaves. When the captain gives the order to row, the officer gives the signal with a silver whistle which hangs on a cord round his neck. The signal is repeated by the under-officers and very soon the fifty oars strike the water as one. Imagine six men chained to a bench as naked as they were born, one foot on the stretcher, the other raised and placed on the bench in front of them, holding in their hands an oar of enormous weight and stretching their bodies towards the after-part of the galley with arms extended to push the loom of the oars into the water and throw themselves back, falling on to the seat which bends beneath their weight.

Sometimes the galley-slaves row for ten, twelve even twenty hours at a stretch, without the slightest relapse or rest, and on these occasions the officer will go round putting into the mouths of the wretched rowers, pieces of bread soaked in wine to prevent them from fainting. Then the captain will call upon the officers to redouble their blows, and if one of the slaves falls fainting upon his oar, which is a common occurrence, he is flogged until he appears to be dead and is then flung overboard without ceremony.

The oarsmen had their heads shaved, with the Buonevoglie being allowed to keep a moustache to distinguish themselves. All of them however started the day with the same drill. At the first whistle they should stand to attention, at the second off caps and shake the vermin out over the gunwales, at the third they do likewise with their shirts, and go on like this through eighteen movements in all.

Galley slaves were treated in the same way by both Muslims and knights. For them it was a system or a way of doing things in those times considering no inhuman element in it, as we all do today. In 1541 the Order had the misfortune to have one of its best knights taken as a slave for the enemy's galleys. Jean Parisot de Valette was wounded and lost his galley *San Giovanni* during an encounter with the Muslim corsair Abd-un-Rahman Kust Aly. He was taken prisoner and sent to the galleys. But then as if fate had already earmarked him for the very important part he had still to play in the Order's history, after a year de Valette was released in an exchange of prisoners between the Order and the corsairs. After going to sea again, in 1554, de Valette had another encounter with the same corsair. But this time it was his turn to take the upper hand and capture Kust Aly who was sent to the oars of the Order's galleys together with his crew.

Birgu was always associated with the slaves since it was there that they were landed when brought over by the galleys. Then they would be taken to the dungeons hollowed out of the rocky foundations of the adjacent Fort St Angelo. A general chapter of the Order held in Malta decreed that provision should also be made for the construction of a regular Naval Dockyard on the shores of Grand Harbour, and this was to be at Birgu. This was to consist of storehouses and slipways under stone arches with wooden roofs where galleys could either be constructed or laid up for refit. From this point the plan was taken in hand and developed until the dockyard of the Order embraced all the foreshore of Grand Harbour. One thing followed another and fortifications were built to the shore establishments that were constructed. In

1545 there was added a bakery with a first floor above it which was utilized as a sailcloth factory. This was the first establishment of its kind of the Order.

It would not be amiss to mention that these establishments continued to be used for the same purpose during the British occupation 400 years later as part of the Royal Navy's Victualling Yard, with the sailcloth factory of course being turned into a Naval Clothing Depot.

These harbour installations and fortifications were completed in good time at a cost which the Order could ill afford. But it was considered to have been money well spent and the grand master might have already been thinking in terms of resting with his laurels and turns his attention to something else when the Muslims struck in 1551. Not at Malta, but at Tripoli which fell to the enemy. Juan de Homedes was furious at the loss, and his anger was directed at the Governor of the dependency Marshal De Vallier whom he sent to prison upon his return to Malta. The truth was that Tripoli had lacked proper defences and as was to be confirmed by de Valette who had been governor there from 1546 to 1549, there had been constant requests made to Juan de Homedes to improve defences which were however never affected. Probably Chevalier Ferdinand de Bracemonte who was governor then between 1541 and 1546 as well as his predecessor the German Bailiff George Schilling, governor from 1535 to 1541 must have done so as well. And De Valliere had done the same but as he was the one on the spot when the catastrophe occurred, he was made the scapegoat.

Being a Spaniard and a compatriot of his Emperor, Juan de Homedes was now terrified of the wrath he expected to fall upon him from that direction, and it might have been this more than anything else that made him turn back to take defensive measures at Malta in case the Muslims would after Tripoli turn their attention to the island. Notwithstanding the harbour defences he had just completed there was still a lot of Malta that was still open and an easy prey to any aggressor. He had only to look at the rocky headland of Mount Sciberras on the side of Grand Harbour opposite Fort St Angelo. There was only a small watch tower and a chapel at the northern end of the long and wide headland, and which could by no stretch of imagination be of any use for defensive purposes. But a proper survey of the situation was made by Leo Strozzi a commander of the Order who made even more alarming revelations of the various weaknesses in the defence of Grand Harbour. The grand master and the Council lost no time and engaged Spanish engineer Pedro Pardo to design a fort to be built at the inner opposite end of St Angelo in such a way that it could combine with same to provide crossfire over dockyard creek where the knights moored their galleys. Work was taken in hand immediately and the fort called St Michael was completed in a reasonably short time.

Pardo was then again engaged to design another fort, this time to be erected on the site of the tower at the northern tip of Mount Sciberras. The design he produced was of another small fort that would also cover that of the second harbour of Marsamxett. It was considered that time was pressing and the design was made in such a hurry that there were some weak points noticed in the plans. They could of course be redone and rectified. But before this could be done there was a raid by Dragut in July 1551.

Dragut Rais was the intelligent and able corsair who spent most of his time fighting and pillaging for Barbarossa. His record of piracy was unequalled and his captives ran into fantastic numbers which also included Maltese who were taken during his previous raids on Malta. This time however, his was not the usual type of raid. Maybe because of the resistance he expected from the knights he took 10,000 men with him, landed them at Marsamxett just beneath the site of the proposed fort and then tried to march round to Birgu and St Angelo. To confront the Turks there was the English Knight Sir Nicholas Upton, by now appointed turcopilier of the English Langue, with 30 knights and 400 mounted Maltese troops. A bloody battle ensued, during which Upton was killed, but although heavily outnumbered, the knights and Maltese gave a good account of themselves in what was the first battle of the Order in Malta. So much so, that finding himself in difficulties Dragut re-embarked his men and sailed north to Gozo where there was nothing to hold him back, and he carried almost all the population of 6,000 into slavery.

This went on to confirm the weakness of the defences to Juan de Homedes and made him hasten the work of the fort without bothering about its weak points that where noticed in the design. Again this fort was quickly completed and was called St Elmo.

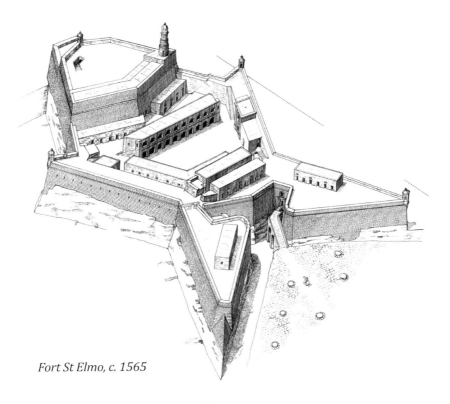

Fort St Elmo, c. 1565

Grand Master Jean de Valette (b. 1494 – d. 1568)

3

GRAND MASTER JEAN DE VALETTE

Changes in human institutions throughout their time of existence had always been inevitable, and there was to be no exception with the Order of St John. But there were also the limitations. The foundation work carried out in Malta by L'Isle-Adam had produced both results and a change. On the approach of the twenty-fifth anniversary of the knights' arrival in Malta the old fishing village of Birgu had been virtually transformed into a busy town which was also extended to another neighbouring community of Bormla. Then although the knights had still not thawed in their relations with the Maltese, they had nonetheless generated bustle and commerce to the island's harbour. Then after Juan de Homedes had built his dockyard, the stores and forts, there was even more work for those who wanted it.

Now, after such time that Maltese had been mostly engaged in agriculture and fishing, the Order began to take them in employment, training them as clerks, storemen and tradesmen. Much as they might have lacked proper education, the Maltese proved to be generally intelligent and quick to learn. They took quickly to Italian, the only language in which they could speak to most of the knights, spiced no doubt by their own semetic language, very often using also Arabic expressions which also disappeared by time. This provided the Maltese not only with a better standard of living but also with a higher level in society. It created a middle class of citizens which never existed, and began to produce artificers and craftsmen that were to become second to none.

As they had done at Rhodes, the knights preferred to recruit seamen for their expanding navy from the locals. And in Malta they found first class material amongst the sea-faring men of Birgu and Bormla. Many of the inhabitants were soon finding work on the galleys as upper-deck seamen, gunners, and sailing masters. Even good for nothing individuals could also mix with the polyglot horde of camp followers who began to gather about the knights for the copious crumbs from their table. Therefore while the nobles and others resident at Mdina persisted in keeping their doors closed against the knights, the ordinary people on the other side of the island and which made the majority became less incensed. To them it seemed as if from a barren forgotten backwater, Malta had started on an era of prosperity. This belief then must have been further strengthened when after the death of Juan de Homedes in 1553, his successor the French Grand Master Claude de la Sengle began to build a new town to adjoin and consolidate Fort St Michael, to be called Senglea after him.

However, the knights themselves would have probably disagreed with such popular feelings, since although they were becoming very particular about Malta, they could not care less about the Maltese, which was of course not the same thing. They had provided work because it paid them to do so to man their public service and their galleys. If they were then providing coast patrols, which impressed the Maltese after they had very often been victims of corsair raids, this was being done with the scope of preventing Muslim corsairs from invading their newly acquired home of Malta. As they had also fought Dragut because it was their vow to fight the Infidel rather than to prevent him from taking slaves.

The truth about the knights was that they had maintained their attitude of aloofness from the Maltese and could not be bothered with them because of another more fundamental reason. Much as they seemed to have turned a new page of their history in Malta they had not changed since their stay in Rhodes, and were still caught up in the tension that had overtaken them in those times when they were in continual confrontation with the ever present menace of the Ottoman Turks, whose empire had since then reached the peak of its glory.

Their aloofness however did not concern women, and some of these were soon becoming the prey of the younger knights, notwithstanding their monastic vows. There was also relaxation when the knights celebrated some particular traditional festivals that had originated and come down from their time in Rhodes. Carnival was one of them which lasted for three days, all full of colour, gaiety in fancy dress and good humour. To which there was now added a new feature of more local interest in the way of a dance called the *Parata* symbolizing the capture of a Maltese bride by a Muslim corsair. The wearing of masks during celebrations then lent scope for the knights to be bolder in their approach to Maltese women, which occasionally caused some trouble.

However, such occasions for relaxation were always brief. And even so, although helping to thaw the knights individually, they never eased the general sense of preoccupation in the Order. At the back of the successful spreading of the Ottoman empire there had been Suleiman the Magnificent, who was the same one who had pushed the Order out of Rhodes. It was true that his run of success had been stopped in Austria when his army was held back at the walls of Vienna in 1529. But this was only to be a temporary setback. And it was an open secret that influential leaders of the Ottoman were still dead intent on a further campaign in Europe differing only as to whether they would strike at Spain or capture Sicily, already being considered as the soft underbelly of Europe. In both options Malta could be involved and with the Order's navy already reacquiring its previous supremacy in the Mediterranean, it would more than likely be considered as a barrier to the Ottoman intentions, that would have to be removed. If this were to happen the Order knew it could not count on any help. Spain and Sicily would be only too bothered to save their own skin, while France was an ally of the Ottoman. There was even much less hope from England where King Henry VIII had strangled the Order with his Reformation. Indeed all Europe was deemed to be in a squabble, and Charles V of Spain, as well as Pope Clement II had already expressed themselves on this matter when as if seeking someone to watch the door against further Ottoman expansion, they had said they needed to look no further than the Order of St John.

But the Order was not in a position to resist an attack from the Ottoman Turks. And the knights knew this. It was indeed this important factor that made them realize that no amount of lamenting would improve the situation, as the state of tension they were gripped in would not keep away an attack by the Turks if these decided upon it. They knew how time and a weak leadership had made them deteriorate in their duties and that they were being considered as having neglected to live in the service of Christ. But now, maybe after an examination of conscience they found out that they were nonetheless prepared to die in His service. But first they had to have the right person to effect their transformation and help the Order recover its ancient authority. And there was only one person who could do this.

It was therefore by universal agreement that on the death of Claude de la Sengle in 1557, they elected de Valette as their grand master.

*   *   *

Jean de Valette was a French noble who had joined the Order at the age of 20 in 1514. His calling had been more of a vocation, no doubt following the example of some of his ancestors who had been knights and fought in the Crusades. The serious intention behind his calling can be better realized from the fact that from the date he joined the Order he had never left the Convent except on his duties. He was strong and handsome and had proved his worth as a fighter in more ways than one. He had had his baptism of fire in Rhodes where he fought bravely throughout the siege, after which he accompanied L'Isle-Adam throughout the Order's stay in Sicily, and its transfer to Malta like the faithful knight he was. He had been inured to the vicissitudes of his calling when in 1541, as had already been mentioned, he was made a prisoner by Muslim corsairs and spent a year as a galley slave. But after his return he spent some time as Governor of Tripoli, and then, until elected grand master he was general of the fleet, a post which was equivalent to that of a commander-in-chief of the Order's navy. He was also appointed bailiff of Largo, grand commander and general prior of St Gilles, and also lieutenant to the grand master. He spoke several languages fluently – Italian, Spanish, Greek, Arabic and Turkish, the last two of which, he learned during the year when he was a slave.

All these qualities were enough to distinguish him from the other knights as a soldier. But then he was also widely known as a hard disciplinarian and a tactician which made him outstanding as a leader. But perhaps the most important thing that could be said about de Valette was that he enjoyed the respect and confidence of all the other knights which was no small thing since it was known all round that he would certainly not tolerate the state to which many of them had sunk. And this made him the man of the moment.

It is a fact that one of the first steps he took on becoming grand master was to transform the knights again to observe the knightly code of living and behaviour to which they had vowed when joining the Order. He prohibited their living outside the confines of their respective Auberges, disallowed duelling, and illegalized drinking and dicing which had crept in and remained unchecked under previous grand masters. Having done this he set out to correct mistakes made by his predecessors. He released Marshal De Vallier whom Juan de Homedes had imprisoned after the fall of Tripoli. Two years later he appointed him grand-bailiff of Largo which was a highly responsible position. He set out to correct the defect that had crept in during the construction of Fort St Elmo at the time of Juan de Homedes. This required the building of an additional ravelin on the Marsamxett side to prevent an approach from that direction to the cavalier and fort. The wood and earth used in this building had to be imported by sea from Sicily. Both the ravelin and the cavalier were then connected with the main fort by a fixed bridge and a drawbridge respectively.

Once he had touched the defences, Jean de Valette then threw himself heart and soul in improving those of Birgu which had of course altered beyond recognition. Bastions were further reinforced with rampant walls and with demi bastions at the ends. The Auberges of the various Langues had been completed and now there began to be built many houses for the increasing population. The already beautiful conventual church was further embellished with the many relics brought from Rhodes. At Fort St Angelo there was also constructed a grain store, while records of the time refer to the places where slaves were kept as slaves' quarters rather than dungeons as they had been previously described. It is not clear whether de Valette had constructed these quarters or used, perhaps with some improvements, the dungeons already mentioned. But whatever it was, the grand master was now using all the slaves the Order had for useful work rather than leaving them to rot in their quarters. It is believed that about 1500 slaves were put to work on the defences, always under the watchful eyes and whips of the knights.

Like his predecessors Jean de Valette lacked the necessary money to pay for the extensive works he was carrying out. But unlike them, rather than hoping or waiting for charity or benevolences, he found ways and means to get what he needed. For many years money was owed to the Order by Germany and Venice who were two of the likely victims if the Ottoman Turks were to resume their offensive in Europe. So de Valette made them realize that since the money they owed him would be used for defences against the common Muslim enemy it would be in their best interests to pay it. His argument prevailed, and the money was paid. It appeared as if the tactful way in which he handled his affairs was producing much precious help and cooperation. Even from the local population who began to see him as the only one who could liberate them from the threat of the island's occupation by Islam.

One sad occurrence which was hurting de Valette and which he could do nothing about was the suppression of the branch of the Order in England. Much as Queen Elizabeth I who had acceded to the throne in 1558 had raised some hopes for the recovery of the Order in her country, nothing had materialized, and indeed there were also some knights, amongst them John Nowell and Edward Walgray who were eventually to die at her hands. By 1560, the English Langue had dwindled to only two knights in the Convent, Oliver Starkey and James Shelley, and all the property the Langue had in Malta had to be sold. It was now that de Valette took Starkey as his secretary and confidante in Malta, and he was never to regret such a wise decision.

Perhaps another quality that distinguished de Valette from previous grand masters was his sense of foresight, .based not as much on his philosophical way of thinking as on his long experience. And in this regard he was more than convinced that the Turks would, in the not too distant future, attack Malta. He knew too that if the Order were to be defeated, it would finish forever, as the Ottoman Turks would certainly not repeat their chivalrous gesture of Rhodes. Christian leaders in Sicily, the Kingdom of Naples and Spain who were by now arguing this point in the same frame of mind, went a step further. They believed that if Malta were to fall to the Ottoman Turks, it would be used for a similarly decisive attack against them, with the likelihood of the fall of Christendom in Europe.

Jean de Valette was now taking no chances, and as from 1563 he began making use of merchants from Constantinople and others who for some reason or other were in contact with the Turks. He got them to spy for him and report any war preparations they might notice on the Turkish side. What he did not know was that the Turks too had sent their spies to Malta, a Sclavonian and a Greek, two renegade engineers who had visited Malta under the guise of fishermen and reported to the sultan of the Ottomans all that was going on in Malta, which made them conclude that the island could not resist a Turkish attack.

Suleiman the Magnificent was well aware of what was going on in Malta, and the report by the latest spies he had sent had only been in the way of confirmation. However, strange as it may seem, the sultan's sense of chivalry and respect for the knights had never abated since Rhodes. In the same way that he had admired L'Isle-Adam after his siege at Rhodes, so he was touched by the way de Valette had brought the Order back on its feet. It was stranger still how this sense of respect never diminished even when in the skirmishes with the Order's navy, his ships continued to get the worst. However, it was after the most recent skirmish by Mathurin D'Aux de Lescourt-Romegas that Suleiman's feeling towards the Order were challenged. Romegas was a swashbuckling knight, well skilled in naval warfare, who was eventually to become general of the Order galleys. In this particular action he captured a Turkish freighter with merchandise worth about 80,000 ducats. But what tickled Suleiman more than the capture of the ship and its merchandise was the fact that this belonged to Kustin-Aga, the chief eunuch of his Seraglio, which as expected started a chain reaction in condemning the constant depredations of the knights. In the process emphasizing the many occasions when during such skirmishes crews and passengers on captured ships were taken as slaves to Malta, amongst them the Sanjak of Alexandria, and the old nurse of Suleiman's own daughter Mihrmah.

As a well-oiled propaganda machine the story and curriculum of the Order of St John continually mocking Islam by the effrontery of its knights gathered momentum by the time scheduled for the Divan or formal council in October 1564. The issue of debate on that occasion was the launching of a large scale military offensive in Europe with the principal aim of expanding the Ottoman empire beyond Hungary and Austria, where its forces had been stopped in 1529. Some favoured an attack on Spain, which was their main Christian adversary, others preferred the capture of Sicily from where it would be easy to proceed against the Kingdom of Naples. It was then that the question of Malta was raised with emphasis being made on the difficulties this island could present if it were to be left alone as it was surely bound to do if not destroyed. Its capture would not only pave the way for the bigger ventures but would also avenge the island's insults on Islam.

If Suleiman was a sentimentalist, he was also a strategist. And although he was not ready to attack Malta for reasons of pique he was swayed to consider such an attack to use Malta as a stepping stone to Sicily, and after that the Kingdom of Naples. Those who had initially been in favour of an attack on Europe agreed and it was then not difficult to reach a unanimous vote. Malta was to be attacked in the spring of the following year.

✳   ✳   ✳

It was not long after October 1564 that Jean de Valette was informed of the hectic preparations that were being made for war by the Ottoman Turks. The feverish activity in the enemy's shipyards and arsenals could not be concealed, and he concluded beyond any shadow of doubt that a sea-borne invasion was being prepared for Malta. As a tactician he knew that an invasion of this sort would not be launched in winter bearing in mind that ships would have to cope with the weather. Moreover an invasion in spring would carry the advantage of a whole summer for an army to consolidate its gains. So he concluded that the Turks would attack sometime in April or May. This gave him a little over six months to make his final preparations.

His first two immediate steps concerned fortifications and an attempt to obtain assistance. He deepened ditches on the landward sides of Birgu and Senglea while he provided larger cannons for Fort St Michael.

There was still a lot to be done, and the island was soon bustling with activity. De Valette delegated all remaining fortification works to the respective commanders while he began to attend to other urgent tasks. There was grain to be brought from Sicily as well as any reinforcements he might be able to obtain from there. He also got in touch with what knights had gone back to their estates or Courts of their respective Sovereigns. 'The Ottoman Turks intend to besiege Malta' ran his general message, 'report to the Convent before spring.' In those days the quickest means of information about enemy landings was by signal fires and preparations were soon taken in hand to erect warning beacons at many strategic points. At Mdina, St Angelo, St Elmo, and in several guard posts along the coast which could not be used for anything else there were piled stocks of fagots and brushwood and men posted at these places to give the signal if and when this was required. There was also a warning beacon erected at the top of Gozo's castle. As he could not hope to have more than between 500 and 700 knights at his disposal de Valette now turned to recruit Maltese irregulars. He found between three and four thousand of them who, although they did not lack courage and also had some experience of skirmishing with corsairs had never experienced long-drawn out warfare. So they were initiated in training on how to handle a musket but were only required to fire three live shots at a target with a premium for the best, because gunpowder had now to be sparingly used.

But even so, de Valette knew that all the forces he could assemble would not be enough unless he received reinforcements from elsewhere. He was already aware that he could not expect anything from France and Germany; one was in an alliance with the Ottomans, and the other was still subjected to ravaging attacks from the Turks and not likely to care about Malta. Queen Elizabeth of England could also be ruled out because of her attitude towards the Order and also of her main concern at the time with the imperial policy of Spain, the more so that Malta was also to a certain extent being considered as a Spanish dependency. Jean de Valette's only hopes lay with King Philip II of Spain, and Don Garcia de Toledo the viceroy of Sicily.

King Philip II of Spain

The first two months of 1565 were even more hectic for the knights with the hundred and one tasks that as always crop up in such circumstances, and with the knights doing them and reporting to the grand master when they were completed. There was the reinforcing of houses in Birgu and Senglea, with also the building of new habitations for the accommodation of new evacuees to those towns; there was also the arrival of the grain brought from Sicily which had to be stored into the great underground chambers, each sealed with its heavy sandstone plug. Barrels of gunpowder and rounds of cannon ball had also to be similarly stored and allocated. From the arsenals there was a continuous flow of suits of mail, whether newly made or refurbished to be redistributed, together with casques and leather doublets to new members of the garrison. There was also the building up of water reserves in the forts by means of thousands of clay water bottles which had to be filled from the natural water springs at Marsa and Mdina and ferried to their destination. Not to Birgu which had its own water supply. There was also the disposition of the galleys to be made. De Valette had already decided that there would be no scope for the Order's seven galleys to be wasted in confrontation with the Turkish armada that was bound to turn up for the attack. So two of them were sent to Messina in Sicily, and three were made secure in the moat behind St Angelo. The remaining two, the *St Gabriel* and *Couronne* were sunk off Birgu from where they could be raised later.

There were general instructions to be issued to the population for all men who could bear arms to rally to the standard of the Order. Those unable to do so which included women, children and old people were to take refuge within the walls of Birgu and Mdina in Malta, while Gozitans were to go into the citadel as soon as the attack began. Farmers were ordered to collect their harvest and take it with them together with their animals to Birgu and Mdina.

As the month of March turned into April, and the Maltese sun became warmer it signified to all that winter was over and spring had well set in. To de Valette however

The fortified landfront of the maritime city of Birgu as it stood in 1565

this meant that all preparations had to be concluded as the day of reckoning was closer. It was time for him to make his dispositions.

He had already decided that the forthcoming battle and siege would have to be fought on land, and with its natural bareness, and with all the crops harvested, Malta could be considered as a natural fortress since the Turks would have to bring all their provisions with them. As for water the one and only available source for them would be a spring and some wells at Marsa. This brought forth a decision from him that the water in these sources will be poisoned when the attack became imminent. A last reassessment of the forces he could dispose of showed de Valette that he had 600 knights and servants-at-arms, and that his original force of Maltese irregulars had increased to between eight and nine thousand. There was neither scope nor hope for anything more. With this force he had to withstand the attack of the Ottoman Turks.

It may here be noted that on the basis of statistics of the Maltese population of that time, nine thousand men must have represented almost half the population of Malta. Considering that the other half consisted of women, children and old people, it will be fair to assume that every able bodied man must have offered his services in the defence of Malta, notwithstanding what a sense of antagonism or ill-feeling there might have been against the knights. It could have been that after having from childhood been inured to the toll so often exacted by Muslim corsairs, the Maltese now wanted to take revenge. But more likely than not it was the positive change in their relations with the knights that made them give their services wholeheartedly in defence of their country.

As Jean de Valette was making his last dispositions on the 9 April he had a pleasant surprise when he was called to the ramparts of St Angelo to see a fleet of 27 galleys of the viceroy of Sicily approaching Malta. His first thoughts were of assistance that must have after all been sent as requested. This belief was strengthened even further when it was known that the viceroy himself, Don Garcia de Toledo was with that fleet. But unfortunately this was not the case. After being welcomed, Don Garcia told de Valette he did not bring any material aid with him. His was only a visit to make him aware that he had asked King Philip II of Spain to send 25,000 infantry troops to Malta which he could not afford to do. The most he promised to send in the near future was 1,000 Spanish foot soldiers. The viceroy also wanted to compliment the grand master on the way he was standing up to the impending attack. He offered some advice on the handling of the situation by recommending de Valette to keep his Council of War to a bare minimum and this to be made up of veterans of war. He also advised the grand master to avoid skirmishes and sorties with the Turks and restrict his action to resist the enemy from pre-laid defences.

Jean de Valette did not need such advice. So much so, that he was already relying on a council as suggested by the viceroy, as he had also already decided to fight the Turks from behind the fortifications of Birgu, Forts St Angelo, St Michael and St Elmo as well as the ramparts of Mdina. He did not need the recommendation of Don Garcia to husband his strength, since this was so limited that he could not do anything else. Nonetheless he listened to the viceroy with his customary patience. Even when he warned him to take care of himself, because his loss could bring defeat. Something the grand master would not consider in the forthcoming circumstances.

As a sign of good faith in the future of the Order notwithstanding its approaching ordeal, the viceroy then left his own son Frederic with the grand master to take the habit of the Order and fight the Infidels.

But before Don Garcia left Malta, de Valette asked him to accept a number of old and infirm Maltese in Sicily so as to have them removed from danger, and at the same time save the Order from having to feed useless mouths. The viceroy agreed and took the first evacuees in one of his ships. Evacuation of some others continued in the following days, but it had then to stop when it was learned that the Turkish armada had left Costantinople. Both de Valette and the Sicilians knew there could be no further sea movements. The moment of truth had arrived.

✳   ✳   ✳

The Ottoman Turks had also made good use of time following the decision taken by the Divan in October 1564 to invade Malta. They had built up an army of about 40,000 men, comprising 6,300 Janissaries who were of the finest troops and all trained arquebusiers, about 9,000 Spahis from Anatolia and Roumania, 4,000 Layalars who were religious fanatics that welcomed death in battle, and the rest being levies and volunteers to make up the number. They were to be carried in a fleet of 130 galleys, and 40 galliots with eleven other big ships each carrying 600 men with 6,000 barrels of gunpowder and 1,300 rounds of canon ball. It had not been that easy to mount such an armada, but the biggest headache for the sultan had been in the appointment of its leaders.

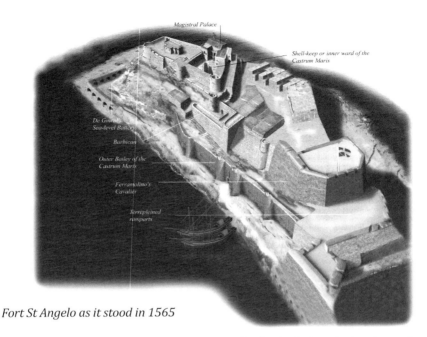

Fort St Angelo as it stood in 1565

Mustapha Pasha, a distinguished general who had already fought against the knights in Rhodes, as well as in the Hungarian and Persian wars was the obvious choice to command the army. He was devoted to the sultan and renowned for his violence and brutality, and was now looking forward to reach the zenith of his career by driving the knights of St John out of the Mediterranean once and for all.

To command the naval element of the armada the sultan appointed Admiral Piali. He was a younger man of Christian parents, but after being abandoned as a child he was brought up as a Muslim in the sultan's seraglio. After making a naval career he was married to Suleiman's granddaughter. There were other outstanding commanders to assist the leaders, like El Louck Aly who was a redoubtable sea-captain and governor of Alexandria, El Louck Aly Fartax a former Dominican brother turned pirate and Muslim, and Hassem, governor of Algiers. But the sultan had reasons to fear that there would be dissension between Mustapha and Piali, so he told them both to wait before beginning the attack until they would be joined by Dragut. The renowned pirate was appointed to join the armada under the pretence of already knowing Malta and de Valette. But the real reason was that the sultan wanted him to watch over his two senior officers Mustapha and Piali who did not see eye to eye in many matters.

On 29 March 1565 the fleet made its way out of the Bosphorus and proceeded to Costantinople where it embarked the army and took stores. From there, watched by the sultan and with great pomp it sailed into the Aegean Sea. It took the armada six weeks to reach the central Mediterranean. On Friday, 18 May it came about 15 miles away from the shores of Malta.

4

THE GREAT SIEGE

The grey and golden hill-sides were then already dappled with the fresh green of the wild grasses and sprinkled with the purple and blue and red of the wild flora. Then as the warm sun rose from the east on that day it struck Fort St Angelo on its back, shedding its silhouette to frolic across the blue water of Grand Harbour.

Beyond the glittering surface of the harbour's main aisle, and past the majestic St Angelo right into the inner end of dockyard creek there was the town of Birgu with its sun-lit buildings and bastions all dominated by the cupola and belfries of the Church of St Lawrence which could be seen rising majestically over the water of the creek. The town had always seen movement and bustle since it housed the headquarters of the knights of the Order of St John of Jerusalem in 1530. But on this wonderful day thirty five years later there was even more movement and people in its narrow streets, which echoed and rang with steps of more than usual armoured men of the Order. All the knights had been called in general assembly to be addressed by their Grand Master Jean de Valette.

It was a very special occasion since this was to be the last meeting before the knights would take their defensive positions for the approaching battle and siege. With all of them in doubt as to whether they would live to see each other again and much less attend another assembly. Jean de Valette spoke to them at length about their duties and the

Turkish galley at the time of the Great Siege

approaching battle. But there were only his last words to be recorded to go into the annals of Maltese history and be remembered again and again every time any reference is made to the knights and their Order.

'It is the great battle of the Cross and the Koran, which is now to be fought. A formidable army of infidels is on the point of invading our island. We for our part, are the chosen soldiers of the Cross, and if Heaven requires the sacrifice of our lives, there can be no better an occasion than this. Let us hasten then, my brothers to the sacred altar. There we will renew our vows and obtain, by our Faith in the Sacred Sacraments, that contempt for death which alone can render us invincible.'

With these last words by their leader, all the knights rose up from their seats exulted and united in spirit, with any private divisions that there might have been between them now disappeared. Then they all marched in procession to their Conventual Church where they received Holy Communion which went further to dissolve any traces of weakness there might have remained. Afterwards they were detailed to their various defensive positions.

De Valette believed that the Turks would attack from the south-east at or near the bay of Marsaxlokk which could also provide a haven for their fleet. But he did not rule out a preference for the northern bay of Marsamxett that was adjacent to Grand Harbour which was certainly to be the eventual fulcrum of the battle and siege. This made it important that Fort St Elmo which covered both harbours should be well manned. Its normal garrison had been of six knights and 600 men under the command of a Piedmontese Knight Luigi Broglia. Now Jean de Valette gave the commander a young Knight Juan de Guaras as his assistant and another 46 knights who volunteered from the several Langues. It happened that two days before on the 13 May there had arrived from Sicily 200 Spanish infantry men of the 1,000 promised by the viceroy. And these were also sent to swell the garrison of St Elmo.

Most of the Order's horses and cavalrymen were sent to Mdina to reinforce the garrison there. Some other reinforcements were also sent to the Citadel in Gozo. The rest of the knights and Maltese infantry units were to remain in the complex of Birgu, Fort St Angelo and Fort St Michael since these could interchange according to the pressure made by the enemy. With these dispositions made de Valette decided to wait for the fateful day. But he did not have long to wait.

The dawn of Friday, the 18 May was as any other. Warm and sunny but nonetheless with the occasional beginning of a sweet cool breeze, so redolent of Spring. Only that a haze had dallied on the water which kept visibility to the minimum. It was when this haze lifted that the sentries at St Elmo and St Angelo got the biggest shock of their lives. Spread out on the horizon where the haze had been, there was the Turkish armada, with the ripples cast by their oars in the still sea indicating a slow but steady approach.

Both St Elmo and St Angelo fired three cannon shots which were the agreed signal, and these were' soon being repeated from Mdina and the citadel in Gozo, to bring the knights, troops and all the population to the alert, just as de Valette had planned.

In the next few hours there was bedlam everywhere. In Birgu and Senglea sailors were trying to organize a reconnoitring force, as the troops and knights on the bastions began seeing to their arms and ammunition. But the organized and silent preparations of the servicemen were soon being distorted by the many farmers who began to arrive with their horses and donkeys loaded with stores and provisions, and their familiars all carrying household goods. Soon inside the walls of Birgu, Senglea and Mdina more than the usual noises of soldiers and armour, there became predominant the bleating of goats and the neighing of horses, and not without the clamour of their own owners. In contrast nothing resembling this was forthcoming from the nobles at Mdina. It's true that they had their houses within the walls and were not expected to ,move anywhere else, but nonetheless it became obvious that they were ignoring the conflict and more than ever before turning their back on the rest of the population around Birgu and the harbour.

It was fortunate that the Turks did not land in Malta on that first day, and this gave the population a chance to settle down. But de Valette availed himself of this opportunity and sent a cavalry detachment to follow the enemy fleet round the coast and report any landing. He also sent men to poison the wells at Marsa. Across the neck of water between St Angelo and Senglea was placed a thick chain to bar the entrance against a sea-borne attack, while he availed himself of the chance to dispatch a small boat to Sicily with a message to the viceroy that the attack had started and he needed help more than ever before.

The Turks began landing at Marsaxlokk by mid-day on Saturday the 19th. They landed about 3,000 men with the intention of capturing what livestock and crops they could find. When they did not find anything they could take, they proceeded towards the village of Zejtun which was a mile and a half away and it was whilst on their way there that they met the first knights' cavalry detachment. A skirmish ensued, but the detachment had to withdraw leaving the first knights to be killed in the encounter. Two knights, the French Adrien de la Rivière and the Portuguese Bartolomeo Faraone were also captured by the Turks and interrogated by none other than Mustapha Pasha. Under torture they were asked to say which was the weakest point in the local defences, and after refusing to say anything, when they could not resist any longer they cried that the weakest point was that of Castile. The truth is that this was the strongest point, and although under torture the two knights had tried to play a trick with Mustapha Pasha.

Even though de Valette did not know this he had noticed how the Turks must have been surprised to find nothing but barren land between the place where they had landed and Birgu and Senglea. This made him conclude that the Turks could now concentrate their attack on the two towns, so he brought all the available foot soldiers from Mdina to Birgu. He was correct for Mustapha Pasha more annoyed than worried by the many skirmishes made by the knights decided to launch a heavy attack on the post of Castile at Birgu.

Jean de Valette was with his knights awaiting the attack, and his orders were for all defenders to stay within the walls and open fire when the enemy came within range. But the multitude of Turks that was seen approaching the post made Christian blood boil. Old and seasoned knights could take it, but for the young ones for whom this was their first action it was different, and before they could be held a number of them got out and ran to meet the advancing infidel horde. De Valette was not pleased but being the wise man he was, decided to let his young knights see for themselves what it meant to be fighting such an enemy. The action would also serve to blood them early. But he could not leave them alone, so he ordered three divisions from Senglea and Birgu to join the young upstarts and engage the advancing Turks.

That action lasted six hours. The artillery from the bastions took a heavy toll of the Turks, but the important fighting was reflected in the clash of steel and the crack of musketry. When he saw the weight of Turkish numbers beginning to tell, de Valette ordered his men to retire. There were only twenty one of his men killed with another 150 wounded. But he could see that there were hundreds of Turks dead on the field. The outcome of this first clash served to raise the morale of the knights and the Maltese that were fighting with them, but on the contrary it annoyed the Turks. As he ordered his men to withdraw, Mustapha Pasha was dead intent to do two things. He would first kill the two prisoners Adrian de la Rivière and Bartolomeo Faraone for having tricked him. Then he would attack Mdina and follow with besieging Birgu and Senglea.

✳   ✳   ✳

The first attack on Fort St Elmo — 27 May 1565

The Turkish commander-in-chief however had been hasty in his last decision, and the moment he expressed his opinion to the council he was immediately overruled by Admiral Piali who was not prepared to leave his supply ships and transports at Marsaxlokk. He suggested transferring the rest of the fleet to Marsamxett on the false premise that there it would be protected from the Gregale or north-easterly wind that often troubled the central Mediterranean. He was wrong on this account because these winds rarely if ever blow after April but Mustapha Pasha did not know this, and on this occasion he was willing to yield to the young admiral. But if they were to take the fleet to Marsamxett they had first to neutralize Fort St Elmo, to which Piali agreed.

Fortunately enough for de Valette it was on that same day that two Christian renegades who were fighting with the Turks decided to change sides and walked to Birgu where they asked to see the grand master. When they did, they told him of the Turks' intentions. They knew about it because one of them was a personal guard to Mustapha Pasha and had been present when the decision was taken.

Jean de Valette reacted by deciding to send further reinforcements to St Elmo. He was lucky again that on that same day there had arrived from Sicily an additional 400 enlisted soldiers under a Provencal Knight Pierre de Massuez Vercoyran popularly known as Colonel Mas. The grand master sent him with half this force to St Elmo, together with 60 freed convicts who had been working as rowers on the Order's fleet, but could be used in defence of the fort. He did this because as he said to Colonel Mas, he believed that St Elmo was the key to Malta.

Was this really so? The Turks seemed to have been of the same opinion judging by the extraordinary efforts

Turkish Sipahis during the time of the Great Siege

that they immediately began making. In the past they had always relied on mining and sapping in attacks of this kind, but in the case of Malta they had come prepared for heavy bombardments, and they had brought big siege guns with them which they now began to carry from the transports with the fleet at Marsaxlokk to be positioned on Mount Sciberras from where they could bombard St Elmo. The transporting of these guns alone was no joke. They had to be carried for a distance of four and a half miles, and the Turks had to use every available animal of burden they had, to drag the cannons over uneven land and primitive dirt roads. When these weapons were in place they spelt terror to the knights. Although these knew that the rate of fire of these cannons was slower than theirs, they knew as well that the battering power of their shot was enormous. The Turks had at least ten of these guns mounted on Mount Sciberras to fire on to St Elmo.

There might have been those who felt that de Valette was very much preoccupied with St Elmo hence his remark about the fort being the key to Malta. But his fears were not as much to losing the fort as to hold onto it until further assistance would be received. And this seems to have been corroborated by the fact that during the attack on the fort he kept sending repeated calls for help to the viceroy in Sicily, the Pope and others. But his requests remained unanswered by all except the viceroy of Sicily who somehow managed to keep contact. But apart from the few hundreds of soldiers he sent which were of little use, he kept asking the grand master to send him the Order's remaining galleys from Malta as if he could not understand that this could not be done because of the Turkish fleet that was besieging Malta, and also that the Order could not spare any men to man the galleys. When the viceroy eventually made his help to the island conditional on the dispatch of these galleys it became obvious that he was only providing an excuse for his inability or unwillingness, whatever it was, to render help. It is no wonder that de Valette when addressing the Council about this matter finally knew that they (the knights) must not look to others for their deliverance, and it was only upon God and their swords they could rely. It was with this premise that the knights and their Maltese companions went into the battle and siege of Fort St Elmo to enact one of the most heroic epics in the history of the Order.

A knight in half-armour during the time of the Great Siege

5

THE FIGHT FOR ST ELMO

The first bombardments of Fort St Elmo began on the morning of 24 May, and right from the start it became evident that the walls of the fort could not withstand the battering power of the Turkish cannons for long. With every hit the lime and sandstone blocks began to powder and flake, and it was not long before the fort's commander Luigi Broglia and his men had to be quick to build further walled protection to breaches that began to appear in the walls. Those who were detailed for this work then, had often to expose themselves to the fire by picked snipers who

The assault on Fort St Elmo

began to shoot with precision at every head or shoulder that appeared above the parapets.

Jean de Valette tried to help by installing two large cannons on a quickly built rampart at Fort St Angelo which could fire directly at the Turkish emplacements across the harbour. Then after two days there was the enemy's reply in the way of a parapet from where guns could fire directly into the besieged fort, with an additional battery which started firing directly on St Angelo. Nonetheless, as this became a triangular artillery battle, it was always St Elmo that got the worst beating. After three days of bombardment the fort's commander Luigi Broglia became so concerned about the number of his casualties that he sent a message to de Valette asking for a continuous dispatch of reinforcements if the fort was to be held. Only that this message was sent by a Spanish Knight La Cerda who through fear or lack of experience painted an even worse picture of the situation at St Elmo. To a question by de Valette as to how long the fort could hold, La Cerda replied eight days. The grand master was enraged, and although he was well aware of the situation he did not want to believe it was so bad just after three days of bombardment, and for a moment he thought it was La Cerda who was exaggerating. Being a master of men's moods de Valette shouted in anger telling La Cerda that he would cross to St Elmo himself at the head of a group of volunteers to hold the fort to the end. More likely than not he had no real intention to do this, but only wanted to give his knights a lesson. When he called for volunteers there were fifty knights who stepped forward even though they knew they would be facing certain death. With them he sent 200 Spanish soldiers all under Chevalier de Medran, to the embattled fort.

The next morning the Turkish batteries continued with their bombardment, but there now appeared to be more purpose behind their firing. This could be attributed to the fact that El Louck Aly the Governor of Alexandria had joined the besiegers, after having brought with him four ships full of stores and ammunition. On the following day however it was the Turks' turn to be shocked when a band of knights and soldiers led by Colonel Mas and Chevalier de Medran dashed out of St Elmo on a sortie and after a brisk fight captured the advanced group of Muslims. The firing and shouting of the fighters could be heard at St Angelo, and de Valette with the senior knights members of his Council watched what was happening from the ramparts. They were obviously overjoyed at this turn out and were soon complimenting each other on the wisdom of sending the last batch of reinforcements. They concluded that after all the defenders of St Elmo were still capable of turning defence into attack.

But their joy was short lived. For Mustapha Pasha too had been surprised by what happened and on leaving his tent he could not believe his eyes on seeing his troops recoil and retreat across the barren heights of Mount Sciberras. Instead of wasting his time in lamenting however, he had immediate resort to his special corps of Janissaries. These specialized troops were always thrown into battle in critical moments, and they always by hook or by crook turned the tables over their adversaries. At the order of Mustapha Pasha hundreds of these soldiers in their white flowing robes with scimitar in hand swept up to meet the knights and soldiers of Colonel Mas and Chevalier de Medran, and it did not take them long to split their ranks. Much as the defenders fought back and contested every inch of ground, they were forced to retreat.

Jean de Valette and the members of his Council saw this setback too from Fort St Angelo. In silence they watched the defenders move back to reach the safety of the fort's gates, with the cannons above them covering their retreat by firing on the advancing Janissaries. In those moments of sombre reflection they might have found some comfort in reasoning that after all the knights and soldiers at the fort had only lost what they had previously gained. But they could not see that the Janissaries had not only recaptured the trenches that had been lost before, but had pressed further forward to capture a parapet above the outer walls which now placed them right into the teeth of Fort St Elmo.

It was not more than two days later when after the first hours of dawn had gone past as others before them there was a mixture of relief from a respite and the sadness of conviction that this would not be for long. As they had done before the knights had during the night carried their sick and wounded from St Elmo by boat to the hospital at Birgu, and made the return trip carrying reinforcements. It happened that one of the wounded on that occasion was the same La Cerda who had become an object of scorn after he had misinterpreted the situation at St Elmo to the grand master. In this instance too when he was examined by doctors his wound was declared to be a superficial one, and the Order's rules permitted no one to be admitted to hospital if he could stand up. La Cerda's behaviour because of fear or cowardice got him a place in the dungeons at St Angelo, instead of the hospital.

But later on that same morning the sudden sound of gunfire brought the defenders of St Elmo and all those in other strongholds out on the ramparts. There was however no evident action at the still smoking fort. On the other hand everyone could see elements of the Turkish fleet outside Grand Harbour, which seemed to be on the move. There were the first thoughts of Sicilian galleys that might have been seen to be approaching Malta, and notwithstanding everything de Valette's thoughts in this regard were of assistance which he was still hoping to receive. But it was soon noticed that the cannons causing the commotion belonged to Piali's ships firing at St Elmo not in anger but more in the way of a ceremonial or show off. But what for? It was only a short time later that there appeared on the scene fifteen galleys which were recognized by their ensign to belong to the squadron of Dragut. As agreed with the sultan, the notorious and able corsair had arrived to join Mustapha Pasha and Piali in the siege of Malta.

Like the consultant the sultan had wanted him to be Dragut did not lose much time. Hardly had he gone ashore that he went straight to the commander-in-chief's tent now located at Marsa, in the open central area that had been occupied by the Turks. With all formalities done away with Dragut asked to be given a picture of the whole situation, but hardly had Mustapha Pasha began to oblige than there was the news received of an attack by two detachments of Maltese cavalry from Birgu and Mdina on a body of Turkish troops near the village of Dingli. Two hundred of the Turks had been killed and the rest put to flight. This piece of news gave Dragut food for thought, particularly when to his further questions he had to be told of other skirmishes between the Order's cavalry and Turkish elements which almost always went against the Turks. Impetuous to get to the point Dragut devoted the rest of his meeting to discuss St Elmo. He disagreed that it should have been the first objective to be attacked. He said he would have preferred an attack on Gozo and Mdina which he presumed to be not so well defended. But with their possession he would have been in a stronger position to prevent boats going to or coming with reinforcement from Sicily. On this matter of reinforcements he specifically told the other two leaders that St Elmo had resisted so long because the knights were allowed to reinforce the garrison by boats from St Angelo. And such communications had to be stopped immediately. But perhaps the greatness of Dragut became evident by the way he did things himself rather than delegating them to others. What dispositions he suggested were to be made after he had personally gone over the ground himself, and checked the information given to him. Then what was even more important he chose to have his quarters in the trenches on Mount Sciberras while he insisted on speak to the troops to hear their viewpoints. He was certainly a man of war and not simply a theorist.

The effect of his presence was felt immediately. The battery on Mount Sciberras was strengthened by 50 guns. A new battery was established at Tignè Point to bombard St Elmo from the north, while he placed another battery at Gallows Point on the side of Grand Harbour. This point was so called because it was there that the knights hanged pirates and criminals, but the place was chosen because the guns placed there could command and cover that part of Grand Harbour between St Angelo and St Elmo, and stop any boats crossing with reinforcements.

Within a day after the arrival of Dragut the firing against St Elmo had doubled. On 3 June his new battery at Tignè Point added to the battering. There was however also an increase in the defenders' firing. Historians very often use the eyewitness account of Balbi da Correggio, an Italian who served throughout the siege and even wrote an eye witness account in Spanish and described St Elmo in those days as being like a volcano in eruption, spouting fire and smoke.

With the advent of June and the approach of the hot summer weather there was added another serious inconvenience to both attackers and defenders not as much because of the shortage of water as to the putrefying stench from corpses of both friend and foe that were piling up in ditches and trenches. The knights collected all their dead in the precincts of the fort and gave them Christian burial but they did not have the means to do the same with the rest, particularly now that every inch of ground outside the fort was in Turkish possession. It was at this time too that dysentery became rife amongst the Turks due no doubt to the poisoning of the wells at Marsa by the knights, and it was at Marsa too that the Turks established a hospital to take and cure both their wounded and those touched by the epidemic.

In the very first days of June the situation seemed to have come to a deadlock. Hampered by the fact that they could no longer receive reinforcements from Fort St Angelo, the defenders had to be more careful where the use of food and ammunition were concerned, as well as the loss of more men other than what they were perforce losing through the continual bombardments. For their part the Turks were itching to attack and conquer the fort and bring this battle to an end, but it was Dragut who was holding them back in expectations of the right moment to risk the picked troops with a good chance of success.

Indeed Dragut was placing his hopes on occupying an important ravelin, and it was only by chance that he did it. It was very early one morning when his engineers tried to inspect this objective. Seeing that they were not challenged by any sentry the two men went forward to peer through a low embrasure. They saw the Christian soldiers inside but they were all asleep. Within a few moments there was an attack launched by the Janissaries, and their screams woke up the sleeping defenders when it was too late. Most of them were killed, but the few who survived owe this to the ingenuity and courage of a knight, Lanfreducci who held the Janissaries by his firing as they stormed forward using ladders and a plank bridge, until the survivors could be let in and the portcullis closed. Nonetheless the Janissaries persisted with their attack, and the defenders by now poised above them replied with muskets and wildfire and fireworks hoops. These fire weapons were made up of highly inflammable mixtures packed into small pots with a fuse. After this was lit, the pots could be thrown to a distance of between 20 and 30 yards with the pot bursting when the fuse reached the explosive and covering a large area with flames. They could be considered as a cross between a hand-grenade of our time and a flame thrower. There were other similar gadgets like the trump which besides belching furious flames also contained a mechanism which fired two small cylinders of iron or brass loaded with gunpowder which in turn discharged bullets. These gadgets were intended for close-up fighting, and in this instance the St Elmo defenders used them with success against the Janissaries when all seemed to have been lost.

Many of the white-robed attackers became human torches while those fireworks missed their target began to land in ditches which the Turks had filled with wood, straw and earth to give them a crossing and access, and now began smoldering to prevent any crossing. With something like 2,000 Turks, mostly Janissaries being killed in this action, Mustapha Pasha stopped the assault and withdrew his men. The defenders had lost only ten knights and seventy soldiers.

✳   ✳   ✳

Notwithstanding this victory for the knights it had to be admitted that the situation had become one that could not go on much longer. Everyone knew it, but no one could say it better than de Valette as he juggled with the dwindling numbers of knights and soldiers from which he had to keep sending reinforcements to St Elmo. His knights, the Maltese and other soldiers had played up, and fought without rest, in the process also suffering hunger, sickness and other privations at the besieged fort, and this always in expectation of certain death. This sequence had become more like a vicious circle which as often happens was doomed to break by human nature. In this case it came near breaking point on 8 June when the grand master received a message from St Elmo by a sealed letter brought by an Italian knight, Vitellino Vitalleschi. It was midnight and de Valette with a premonition of trouble opened and read the letter by candlelight. It was more of a petition signed by fifty-three knights which started by describing in detail the situation at St Elmo which they had defended with the greatest of good heart without sparing fatigue and danger. However the enemy had reduced them to such a state that they could neither fight him any longer nor defend themselves. As they were convinced the fort was sure to fall, the petitioners asked to have boats sent to them so that they could withdraw to fight another day. If this could not be done they were prepared to sally forth and die as knights should.

For a few moments Jean de Valette stood looking in silence at the letter in his hands, burdened with heavy thoughts. The request could not be classified as mutiny. The petitioners who like they said had been subjected to the worst kind of fighting and bombardments were only asking to be allowed to preserve themselves obviously to keep on fighting somewhere else rather than die hopelessly, however honourably. Nonetheless de Valette knew he had a revolt on his hands and of all places at St Elmo, and at its most delicate time. The request wanted a quick decision which he was not prepared to take there and then. He needed time if he was to find a way out. He called three knights from different Langues and told them the gist of the request. Then he asked them to cross over to St Elmo and report on its state. 'Our Laws of Honour cannot be satisfied by throwing away one's life when it seems convenient,' said de Valette to Vitellino Vitalleschi, 'a soldier's duty is to obey, and tell your comrades that they are to stay in their posts and not to sally forth. I will decide what is to be done, when I receive a report on the fort's situation.' Indeed the delegated knights, Knight Commander Medina, Antoine de la Roche, and Costantino

A sixteenth century engraving depicting the salient episodes of the Great Siege, May – September 1565 by Matteo Perez d'Aleccio

Castriola went to St Elmo as bidden and returned on the same day. Two of them reported that they considered the position at the fort to be hopeless, but the third one was optimistic that with a few more reinforcements the fort could be held for some more time. Then he volunteered to lead such reinforcements himself. True to his word after obtaining the grand master's permission, Castriola mustered about 600 men who were prepared to go to St Elmo's relief.

Jean de Valette could certainly not dispose of so many men. But his was only a psychological move to help his revolting knights to regain their sense of pride. Immediately he sent another message to them saying that a volunteer force had been raised and that they could withdraw from the fort when this new force would take over. He did not fail to add that while they would then be more secure on their return, he would also benefit by henceforth having the fort defended by men he could trust. His plan worked for within minutes of receiving his letter the knights realized that if they were to carry on with the threat and withdraw they were bound to be branded as the men who saved themselves but lost St Elmo. Their sense of honour as knights prevailed over their sense of preservation. So they replied to the grand master by a letter which they sent by the swimmer Toni Bajada. In it they begged the grand master not to relieve them and promised to fight to the end at St Elmo.

De Valette forgave them and as a sign of his forgiveness he sent 10 knights and a few score of soldiers to help the defenders of St Elmo.

✳   ✳   ✳

During those first days of June Jean de Valette was not the only one to be assailed by worries about the battle for St Elmo, because the recent exploit by the defenders seemed to have mesmerized even the great Dragut. Much as the fort had almost been razed to the ground, the knights, Maltese and other soldiers had continued to resist, and it was no secret that the Turkish High Command had concluded that the battle was going badly. To make matters worse for them, a knights' cavalry detachment under Marshal Copier who had already distinguished himself in many cavalry charges, now attacked and destroyed Dragut's battery at Gallows Point. And this made it possible again for the knights to send boats with reinforcements to St Elmo across Grand Harbour. Mustapha Pasha then was more than perturbed as he began to fear the arrival of bigger reinforcements for the knights from Sicily which would spell the end of his operations. It is no surprise then that he had the biggest shock of his life when on the 10 June, which was also the date for an intended new attack, two Maltese galleys appeared off the north of Gozo.

Mustapha Pasha assumed that those galleys were the advanced part of a bigger fleet and he quickly asked Piali to intercept. In truth those were the original two galleys that de Valette had sent to Syracuse before the siege started. Now they had been sent back by the viceroy of Sicily with 500 soldiers in response to the grand master's continual requests for help. The soldiers aboard were all the viceroy could provide at the time, but even so they were not landed as Piali was quick to chase them off. Following this Dragut intervened and insisted that henceforth a hundred of Piali's ships should patrol the Malta Channel in order to intercept any other ships with assistance for Malta. He also asked for another and much stronger battery to be erected at Gallows Point as he also wanted to have small boats with armed men in Grand Harbour to intercept what similar boats of the Order tried to run the gauntlet with reinforcements for St Elmo during the night. This made the defenders at St Elmo have more resort to Maltese swimmers to carry messages to St Angelo during the night, and this became the only means of communication with Grand Master Jean de Valette. With all these loose ends believed to have been tied up, the Turks could carry on with their intended attack which they were hoping would be the last and conclusive one on St Elmo. The Aga and leader of the Janissaries spoke to his men before sending them into action. This time, he told them, they had to capture the fort, and slaughter all the infidels, meaning the Christians. For the first time the attack was to be delivered at night on that same day of 10 June.

Guided by the light of torches and fireworks the Janissaries threw themselves into the assault. According to the historian Balbi, the glare was such after fighting had started, that the darkness of night became bright as day. St Elmo was so illuminated that it could clearly be seen from all localities in the harbour area. This of course included St Angelo from where the Order's gunners could train their guns on the attacking Turks. It was another terrific battle with the attackers storming the fort several times only to be beaten back. When dawn broke and fighting stopped the Turks had something like 1,500 of their men killed. The defenders had only 60 dead.

But now there was to be no pause. The Turks were so enraged by the way their attack had been beaten back that any initial thought for pause and planning disappeared. Bombardments and fighting continued for a further three days and it was only stopped so that Mustapha Pasha could on the 14 June offer the defenders a safe and unmolested passage if they were to surrender. The man who carried that message had to run back for his life from the hail of arquebus shot at him. So the bombardments were resumed with the added firing of Piali's ships in anticipation of another attack that was launched on 16 June.

This time Mustapha Pasha threw the Layalars in front, who, maddened by hashish knew no fear as they also disregarded completely both their life and that of others. As they were further incited by the mullahs the one word that was on their lips was that of 'allah', as the Maltese in the defenders' ranks must have similarly called on 'Alla' for help. The two words both referred to God.

The defenders that were left in the fort even now were huddled together as if to take courage from each other's presence. Saying their last prayers they aimed their weapons at the frenzied wave of Layalars moving towards them. At the right time a small battery of cannon opened up on them pointblank. Then muskets and arquebus began taking toll of those who kept coming. When before there was time to reload and some of the Muslims reached the breaches in the walls the knights waiting there had to resort to lances and swords to ward off the Layalars with their round shields and scimitars, and when these stood fast in the breaches then the knights mixed with them in deadly battles.

Every Christian taking part in that battle fought with the premise that his end had come since by no stretch of imagination could he believe that the enemy would be overwhelmed. Yet there was a moment when the Layalars stopped and retired. It was unbelievable and many a Christian was thinking in terms of a miracle. But this pause as many others before it lasted enough for the defenders to take breath, reload and recoup. When they had hardly done all that there was another assault, this time by the Janissaries. These were met with a similarly concentrated fire of cannons, and then again by muskets and arquebus. Unlike the Layalars these found the time to stop and regroup, but in their attacks they never went beyond the breached walls. The valiant defenders saw to that.

Both Dragut and Mustapha Pasha supervised this operation, as they also maintained a continuous bombardment. But when night fell they had to call it off with both sides justifiably unable to believe how the fort had resisted the attacks. It was also incredible how the defenders had lost only 150 men to the Turkish dead which numbered over 1,000. Jean de Valette was proud of his men, but he felt that the time had come to stop sending any more reinforcements. Yet there were 30

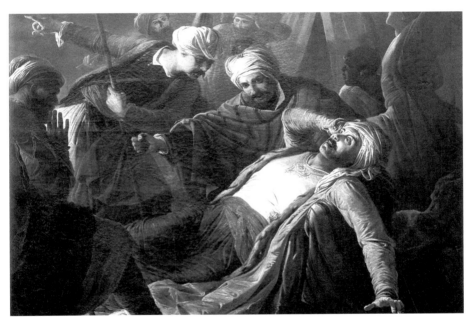

Painting of The death of Dragut *by Giuseppe Calì*

knights and 300 soldiers and Maltese who volunteered and offered themselves to go and die with those who were still holding fast at St Elmo.

On 18 June Dragut and Mustapha Pasha were busily engaged in supervising further improvements in anticipation of their next assault. The battery at Gallows Point was now dominating the harbour to prevent transport of reinforcements, but there was also erected a screening wall right to the water's edge sealing St Elmo from the outside world. This was also Dragut's idea, but he was not to see it working for a cannon shot from St Angelo fell quite close to him and he was struck behind his right ear by a great splinter of rock thrown by the shot. He fell to the ground with blood gushing from nose and ears. Mustapha Pasha who was near him assumed he was dead, but without much ado had him covered quickly with a cloak, and had him taken secretly to the hospital at Marsa. He did not want anybody to know of his death fearing that the troops would be demoralized. A short time later a similar shot killed the Aga and leader of the Janissaries. It seemed as if the gunners from St Angelo were deliberately aiming at important leaders where they could be identified by their flashy clothes.

*   *   *

The news that Dragut was killed reached the grand master through a deserter from the Turkish army. However he was then not yet dead, because after he was found to be still alive at the hospital he lingered on before he died some days later. But even so during the time he remained alive he could not be further involved. What measures he had recommended however were carried out by Mustapha Pasha. On 20 June the new battery at Gallows Point began to dominate Grand Harbour. When it was not preventing reinforcements to be carried to St Elmo it could train its guns on the eastern side of the besieged fort. There was by now also completed the screening wall which sealed the fort from the outside world. On this same day a last message from St Elmo informed de Valette that there was no further scope to send reinforcements as the fort was as good as lost. It was of course all superfluous, since the fort was now cut from everything and everyone and had to carry on alone.

*   *   *

The 21 June was a day of contrasts. In Birgu where notwithstanding the situation the Order was celebrating the feast of Corpus Christi, there was a look of calmness. The knights had put aside their arms and armour and wore their ceremonial dark robes with the white eight-pointed cross as they took part in the procession, and the ceremony at the conventual church of St Lawrence. It was also programmed that from the morrow there would start the preparations for the traditional bonfires to be lit on 24 June when it would be the feast of St John, the patron saint of the Order.

In St Elmo where the Turks had persisted with their attacks the situation had become precarious. All order of battle had disappeared. What Christian guns still functioned would fire point-blank at the charging Muslims causing heavy casualties. And so would the musketeers and arquebusiers, but with every wave dispersed, another would take its place until the breaches in the walls are reached. Fighting would then devolve in face to face mortal combat using two-handed swords, scimitars, pikes, battle-axes and even daggers. The battle would sway back and forth, and there would be the night when fighting will stop to be resumed at dawn.

Luigi Broglia the fort's commander was incapacitated by wounds, so Melchior de Monserrat, a knight of Aragon took over. It was not long before he too was killed by

The fall of Fort St Elmo, 23 June 1565

a musket shot. Colonel Mas, de Guaras and Miranda, three stalwarts of St Elmo were badly wounded, but continued fighting. When they could no longer stand they had themselves placed in chairs in the breaches, to fight with their two-handed swords. When de Valette learned of their plight he cried and wanted so much to send another volunteer force as reinforcement. There was no lack of volunteers and to lead them stood forward the firebrand Romegas. But when they tried to cross over they were prevented from doing so by the Gallows' Point battery and also Turkish patrol boats. There was nothing else that could be done.

In the meantime the defenders of St Elmo continued to fight. No thought of surrender crossed their minds. De Guaras had his head struck off by a scimitar and Colonel Mas was cut to pieces. Miranda was dead too as were other valiant knights. When on the 23 June the whole of the Turkish fleet moved to Marsamxett and added its weight to the bombardment there was a further onslaught by Janissaries, Spahis, Layalars and Levies. To face them there were less than one hundred defenders. The two chaplains Ouerre Vigneron a French, and Alonso de Zambrana, a Spaniard who had been at the fort from the beginning of the siege confessed the remaining knights and soldiers, and gave them Holy Communion. Then after hiding precious sacred objects and burning everything in the chapel they began to ring the bell. This was the signal to the rest of the knights across the harbour, that St Elmo had reached the end.

Indeed, on that day of 23 June, the eve of the feast of the Order's patron saint, St Elmo fell. Mustapha Pasha had little cause for joy when he went over the ruins of the dead fort. At one stage then his gaze turned to the fort of St Angelo, across the harbour and he made the famous exclamation that was not to be left out by any historian.

'Allah' he said. 'If the daughter has cost us so much, how much will we have to pay to get the mother?'

6

A BATTLE FOR SURVIVAL

There were many unexpected illuminations in Malta on the night of 23 June. Notwithstanding the gloom because of the loss of St Elmo, the knights lit their traditional bonfires at Birgu, Senglea and Mdina in celebration of the feast of their patron St John on the morrow. But the Turks also lit their own bonfires to celebrate the capture of the Christian fort.

On the following morning the bright sun shone from a blue sky, but the warm aura of summer which always enhances the beauty of Grand Harbour was this time marred by what bastions and buildings that were pockmarked after .the thirty-one day siege of St Elmo which had ended the previous day. And to drive in this sad recollection there was the Turkish crescent over the ruins of the fort flaunting in the breeze which also generated a slight current that swept through the entrance of Grand Harbour. But floating with this current on that calm morning there appeared three contraptions made up of cross-beams of wood in the form of crucifixes. And nailed on to them there were the headless bodies of three knights.

Jean de Valette was with his council at that moment, but he was called immediately to see the ghastly contraptions which had in the meantime been washed ashore beneath Fort St Angelo. Two of the bodies were recognized to have been of Jacomo Mortelli and Alessandro San

Headless bodies of the knights on rafts

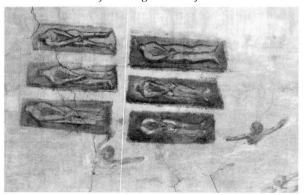

Giorgio, two Italian knights. Coming after another bizarre act by Mustapha Pasha when he had stuck the heads of Colonel Mas, Miranda and de Guares on stakes at St Elmo and made them to face St Angelo, de Valette seems to have lost control of his well known sense of affability which had been considered so extraordinary in that rough age. He retaliated immediately with another bizarre act when he ordered all Turkish prisoners to be decapitated, and their heads catapulted into the enemy lines. Even so, it must have been his angry excitement rather than anything else that made him act in this way.

The grand master had reason to refind his calm later that day when he learned that some reinforcements had arrived and managed to land stealthily in Malta. It was a force of about 700 men sent by the viceroy of Sicily in four galleys whose naval commander however was given the express order that they were only to be landed in Malta if St Elmo was still in the knights' hands. If not, the force had to be taken back to Sicily. When the galleys anchored in the north-west of Malta, a knight was put ashore to find out about the situation. He learned that St Elmo had fallen but rather than informing the naval commander, he chose to inform only the leader of the group Chevalier de Robles, who in turn not to deprive the Order of this much needed reinforcement deceived the naval commander by telling him that St Elmo still belonged to the knights and was thus allowed to land his force. Then he managed to lead them to the shores of Kalkara creek where they found boats to take them to nearby Birgu.

The Turks learned about these reinforcements when it was too late to intercept them. Then they didn't know there had been only 700 men and were indeed led to believe there were more. Mustapha Pasha had still not got over the fact that he had to waste so many thousands of his men at St Elmo, and was already feeling uneasy about continuing with the siege. Perhaps more than uneasiness it was a nervous irritability he was feeling about having to eventually face Suleiman and tell him of the high price in lives, armour and reputation he had to pay in pushing the knights out of Malta. It was in turn this fear that began tickling him to do what the sultan himself had done forty three years ago at Rhodes. If he were to offer the knights a safe conduct out of Malta he would still have achieved his main scope without incurring any further losses. He became so enthusiastic about the idea that he forgot about the atrocities he had committed with the knights and soldiers he had captured at St Elmo, and how he had mocked the knights' Catholic religion by crucifying their headless brethren and putting them onto the water of Grand Harbour. But whatever were his feelings he was underestimating de Valette. He chose a Greek slave of Christian parentage to carry his message to Birgu under a flag of truce. After the grand master listened to what the messenger had to say, he said to those around him: 'Take him away and hang him.'

Jean de Valette did not mean what he said. His was only a shock tactic to subdue the man. So much so that after agreeing to let him live he had him taken to be shown the fortifications of Birgu which left the messenger looking in awe. Then de Valette showed him the ditch and told him that was the only place he would give Mustapha Pasha and his Janissaries.

The Turkish commander-in-chief was furious when he received this message

The siege of Fort St Michael, 27 June 1565

from his messenger. He realized immediately how foolish he had been to expect any form of surrender from the knights. If there was to be anything they would have to concede, it would have to be taken from them by force. It was this that made him put away all his doubtful contemplations, and decide to attack Senglea, Fort St Michael and Birgu. He assumed that if he conquered those places, St Angelo which would then be the only remaining stronghold would fall like a ripe plum.

*　　　　*　　　　*

Mustapha Pasha was in agreement with the knights that no ship could pass the heavy guns of St Angelo, and he therefore hit upon a plan of how he could bring his ships in harbour and in a position to attack his objectives without risking being sunk by St Angelo's artillery. He decided on an old strategy, namely of taking a number of large boats across the land from Pietà Creek to the inner parts of Marsa. Strange as it might have seemed, for the next few days he put every slave he had to work in pulling the boats ashore at Marsamxett and then carry them to the leeward end of Mount Sciberras. From there he could slip them towards the sea at Marsa where they would be in a position to attack Senglea and Fort St Michael without being a target for the guns at St Angelo. When 10 large boats were transported in this way to Grand Harbour, Mustapha Pasha took more heavy artillery to Mount Sciberras, as well as to Corradino Heights from where he could reach his targets even more easily.

When de Valette realized what the Turks were doing he could not help admitting it was an astute plan, so he produced another one of his own to prevent enemy ships from landing any men on the peninsula of Senglea and St Michael. He gave orders for a palisade to be built from the tip of Senglea to the end of the fortifications. This was to be made of stakes bound at the top with iron hoops, and driven into the sea bottom. A similar palisade was to be built at Kalkara creek to protect Birgu from its northern side.

The Turkish bombardment opened at the end of the first week of July, and the towns of Birgu and Senglea as well as forts St Angelo and St Michael were the targets. Although his ships had been hauled into their proper alignment for the bombardment, Mustapha Pasha knew he had to destroy the palisade round Senglea and St Michael if he was to land his troops, so he sent some picked swimmers armed with axes and hatchets to do the job. These had swam half their way across the creek when Admiral del Monte the commander of Senglea was informed of what was happening. He was taken by surprise because no provision had been made for such a contingency. He had no organized swimmers in his battalions, and it was an age when few men, even sailors, were swimmers. But this did not apply to the Maltese who being natives of a small island learned to swim from childhood. At their commander's call, a number of Maltese armed with knives and stabbing swords ran to the water's edge, took off their clothes, and threw themselves into the sea. They then swam with their weapons between their teeth to reach the Turkish swimmers just as they began to cut down the palisade. Maltese and Turks met in a hand-to-hand combat, but it soon became evident that the Maltese were more than a match for the Turks who quickly retreated leaving at least one dead and carrying others that were wounded with them.

There was a second attempt by Mustapha Pasha to destroy the palisade on the following day. This time by securing ship's ropes to the stakes which were taken back to capstans on the shore of Corradino. The Turks had only to wind their side of the rope to drag out sections of the palisade. But Maltese swimmers again took to the water this time to cut the Turkish ropes and release pressure on the palisade which was saved. Mustapha Pasha now decided there were to be no further attempts on the palisade. The time had come for his major attack on Senglea and St Michael. He agreed to allow Hassem, the viceroy of Algiers who had joined him to lead the attack. He would lead the assault on Senglea while his lieutenant Candelissa would try to invade St Michael. The combined attack was launched on 15 July.

Right from the start the attack on Senglea and Fort St Michael appeared to be more organized than that on St Elmo. Mustapha Pasha and the other leaders proceeded as planned with the assault.

It fell to Candelissa to throw his men against the palisade, and for some time his boats had to stop because of these defences. It was however enough to permit the Christian musketeers to open a deadly fire on the Muslims. This did not deter the agile Candelissa from throwing himself into the water and order his troops to follow him covering their heads with their shields from the musket shooting and what was being thrown at them from the ramparts. They suffered many casualties but what troops managed to wade to the shore were soon preparing to escalate the walls.

Hassem too, who was leading his own Algerian troops was soon trying to do the same thing against the walls of Senglea but in his case he found the going much heavier

The barrage against the ottoman boats from from de Guiral's battery and Senglea Point

because of some well placed artillery under the command of Chevalier de Robles who had led the latest reinforcements to Birgu, and was causing havoc to his troops. Even so some of these managed through sheer courage to reach the parapet where the knights met them in face-to-face combat.

There was a lucky break for Candelissa when a Christian powder magazine on the Senglea side blew up and opened a wide breach in the bastions. His troops did not lose time and jumped into this breach. Then after the dust and smoke cleared away everyone could see the Turkish banners that were placed on the walls of Senglea. Realizing that the town could easily fall, de Valette immediately sent reinforcements from Birgu. These had only to run across the bridge of boats he had built from the town. In the counter attack that followed led by Commander Zanoguerra the enemy's advantage was neutralized. The defenders had to extend themselves to do it but amongst them there was no division, and even their chaplain Fra Roberto who was not expected to bear arms or fight, on this occasion pulled up his cassock to the waist and charged with the troops.

As Mustapha Pasha watched the ebb and flow of this battle from Corradino Heights he felt the time had come for him to send in his Janissaries who could certainly turn the scales in his favour. One thousand of these troops in ten boats made straight for Senglea from the water's edge at Mount Sciberras, but they were not to reach their objective. A battery of guns at St Angelo under the command of a Knight De Guiral opened fire on these boats and destroyed nine of them before they could reach Senglea. The remaining boat had to return back.

The battle raged for five hours but the Algerians and Turks were soon feeling the losses of men they had incurred which amounted to about 3,000. They were told to retreat and in the confusion had to leave many of their soldiers behind who could not reach safety in time. When these tried to surrender they were still killed by the defenders of Senglea and St Michael who were not prepared to let no quarter after remembering all that had happened at St Elmo.

✳   ✳   ✳

But Mustapha Pasha remembered St Elmo too, and amongst other things how the defenders there had been able to hold on because of the reinforcements that de Valette managed to send them constantly. This could be done much easier now because of the bridge that had been built between the peninsula and Birgu. He realized immediately he would have to stop this flow of reinforcements if he were to have any success. He knew it was impossible to go for this bridge being as it was too deep inside the creek, and also defended by the chain that had been put across. There was also the fact that the creek was covered by a terrible cross-fire from both sides. So the Turkish commander-in-chief hit upon another idea. If he were to attack Birgu at the same time he was invading the Senglea and St Michael peninsula the knights would not be in a position to spare any reinforcements to cross over. It was a good stratagem and he liked it.

However there was another psychological move Mustapha wanted to try. Now that his attacks were to involve the civilian population he thought of the possibility of driving a wedge between the Maltese and the knights. And this he tried to do through propagandists who promised the Maltese freedom and fair treatment if they detached themselves from the knights and gave up the struggle. But this showed how much Mustapha did not know the Maltese. They had by then already left a clear imprint on history of their love for freedom always based on their devotion to church and religion. For these ideals they had already arisen against oppressors in their long history of feudalism. Then there was their traditional characteristic of unification whenever they were faced by danger of attack. So even though they did not see eye to eye with the knights, in the prevailing circumstances they preferred to be ruled by the knights rather than being the companions of the Turks. Mustapha's offer was rejected, and

'Gardjola' (watch tower) at Senglea Point

when there was only one man, an Italian soldier who expressed the opinion that the Turkish terms should be accepted he was taken to the ramparts and hanged.

Mustapha started his two pronged offensive with a bombardment as had never been seen before. We have it from writers of that time that the sound of Turkish gunfire could be heard like thunder in Sicily, 100 miles away, and the harbour area looked more like a volcano erupting flames and smoke. Anticipating the attack on Birgu, de Valette began constructing fresh stone barriers in that town, using all the slaves he had to do the work quickly. Some of them fell victims to the bombardment, and those who tried to refuse doing the work were put to death. Anyone showing just a disinclination to disobey orders had his ears cut off. It had become a race against time since de Valette was expecting the attack at any hour. Indeed Mustapha Pasha had now decided to lead the attack on Senglea and St Michael himself, while Admiral Piali was entrusted with the operations against Birgu. Candelissa was given command of the fleet cruising off the entrance of Grand Harbour. His last move was to install a new heavy battery on Bighi point just opposite Birgu from where the town could be subjected to an immense weight of fire. Then he launched his assault on 2 August.

From every slope and ridge the Turkish forces swept like tigers against the walls of the two garrisons. There were at least five occasions when Mustapha's troops managed to scale the walls of St Michael, and at least on one occasion they were fighting inside the fort. But on each occasion they were pushed back by savage counter-attacks. Birgu held fast. But after five hours it was Mustapha's turn to be disappointed when he saw that notwithstanding everything, the banner of St John was still flaunting on the ramparts of Birgu, Senglea and St Michael. His efforts with the great loss of men involved had all been in vain. So he stopped the attacks and decided to bombard his targets for a further five days before he would launch another assault.

The truth is that his efforts were not completely in vain. Senglea had been torn to rubble, and so was Birgu. The battle had been taken to the civilian-population. Men, women and children who had until then endured the siege in silence and prayer were made to realize the end was near and they just couldn't be expected to await death. Until then their sense of defiance had made them hope. But hope for what? The defenders were becoming fewer and every pair of hands had to do the jobs of ten. Everyone realized how he or she could help, and if they were to die it would be better to die fighting. At first it was a trickle, but there soon was an exodus of men, women and children to join the members of the garrison on the ramparts and in their forts. There were breaches to be repaired, barriers to be built in the streets, food and ammunition to be carried, and wounded to be tended to. Every able bodied Maltese in Birgu and Senglea had overnight become a part of the garrison.

The assault was renewed on 7 August. Piali's men had burst into a breach in the ramparts of Castile at Birgu and surged forward for the kill only to be faced by another wall, one of the many de Valette had just built. By the time they realized they had gone into a trap they found themselves under heavy fire to be slaughtered in hundreds. It was now the turn of knights and soldiers to take the offensive and with sword, lance or pike in hand these leapt at the Muslims to turn their advantage into a rout. And Piali could not but watch his men stagger back from the walls of Birgu and run for the safety of their lines.

It was however a different story at Senglea and St Michael. The Muslims had stormed a part of the wall and penetrated into the citadel. It was now the grand master's turn to watch painfully the wavering line of Turkish pennants being stuck on the bastions of St Michael, while he could not send a single man from Birgu in the way of reinforcement because of the battle still raging there.

With sword in hand seventy-year-old Mustapha Pasha himself could be seen leading his forces, as the knights and soldiers began to fall back. The battle for Senglea and St Michael was as good as lost, and to drive his advantage further in, Mustapha called in the Janissaries for the final stroke. The knights, soldiers and the civilian population had always laid their hope in God and the Blessed Virgin. Theirs was a strong faith which never relaxed throughout the siege, but it was in dire moments like this that their steadfast belief made them hope for the impossible and miraculous. And this time it happened.

With their backs to the wall, knights and soldiers stood with sword in hand ready to meet the onrushing Janissaries. Their last moment had come, when suddenly above the noise of battle they heard the Turkish signal for their soldiers to retreat. It was unbelievable how only a question of minutes away from victory, Mustapha could have called back his troops. But theirs was not a dream, because indeed the Muslims gave up what ground they had conquered and began to withdraw quickly from the fort. Another amazed person was de Valette who from Birgu watched the unexplained Muslim retreat. What had been the cause of it all?

It had all started with Chevalier Mesquita, the Governor of Mdina. He and his garrison had long waited almost in idleness at the capital for the attack that did not materialize. When he knew about the Turks he felt he had to do something. Some say it must have been an inspiration. Whatever it was, Mesquita dispatched the whole of his cavalry force under Chevalier de Lugny to attack the Turkish camp at Marsa. There was little if any resistance by the Turks, since the hundreds if not thousands of Turks there were in the hospital, were casualties with only a small guard of sentries who were certainly no match for the Order's cavalry. In a very short time the angry knights had massacred every Turk they found there and destroyed the camp.

The only one to escape their wrath was a lone horseman who rode hell for leather to Mustapha Pasha and informed him that a large Christian force had devastated the camp at Marsa, and killed every soldier there. Knowing that all Christian forces were concentrated at Birgu, Senglea and St Michael, Mustapha assumed that reinforcements from Sicily must have arrived and taken him in the rear. And that was the reason why he called off the attack.

7

THE MIRACLE OF COURAGE

The news of Malta's and her knights' plight and courage had travelled fast all over Europe. There was praise and admiration forthcoming from everywhere, but no one lifted a finger to send badly needed help. The biggest failing in this regard could be attributed to the viceroy of Sicily, who notwithstanding his promises of help to Jean de Valette, had only sent one small force as reinforcement. To make matters even worse, now that this matter had generated some hot discussions in the viceroy's court, there was an element in this same court which was against sending any help to the knights, even at the cost of having Malta abandoned to be occupied by the Turks.

There were arguments that the knights were not subjects of Philip II of Spain and were therefore not entitled for such help. There were also references made to the knights' downfall in Rhodes, when no European monarch had helped them, and it could therefore not be expected that the Spanish Emperor should do so now. However Don Garcia, the viceroy, did not agree with such arguments. He believed that as Malta was a Spanish gift to the knights it merited Spain's assistance in her hour of need. But even so, he reminded those around him that Sicily was already being threatened by the Ottoman Turks from Budapest and Belgrade in the north, with the west having been blocked by France after her treaty with the Turks. The eastern side was dominated by the Muslims, and this left only the south with Malta's fate being in the balance. If the island fell, it would no doubt be used as a stepping stone by the Turks for an invasion of Sicily. This was of course an old argument which had never been heeded by the viceroy himself, but now the indomitable heroism of Malta and the knights was pressing upon him a feeling of shame.

This made him send another message to de Valette with another promise that by the end of August he would send 24 galleys and 14,000 men to his assistance. But what Don Garcia seemed to have not considered was whether the knights and Maltese would survive until then.

In Malta Mustapha Pasha had in the meantime laid down the plans for his next and what he expected to be the final assault. He would attack Senglea but not Birgu.

This, he thought, would entice de Valette to send reinforcements as he had always done with St Elmo, and this would deplete his garrison at Birgu. He had now also decided to have resort to his old tactic of burrowing and laying a mine beneath the strong bastion of Castile at Birgu to be exploded at the opportune time and catch the defenders by surprise. Even if this were to fail he had by now built a large siege engine made up of a tower and drawbridge which could be used by his soldiers to climb over the ramparts' walls and right into the town itself.

The Turkish commander-in-chief waited until his engineers told him they had burrowed and placed the mine under the bastion of Castile, on the 18 August. On that same day he launched his attack on Senglea which developed as on previous occasions. Then he kept a strict watch on what was happening at Birgu.

As always Jean de Valette was inclined to send some reinforcements from Birgu to Senglea, the more so when he saw that the garrison there was hard-pressed. But the fact that Birgu was not attacked made him wary. He immediately suspected that some trick was being played by the Turks, and therefore against his wishes he refrained from sending any more troops over. This did not escape Mustapha Pasha's attention who immediately realized that the grand master did not fall into his trap. So without waiting any further he ordered his engineers to blow up the mine beneath the bastion of Castile. When it went off, there was a gigantic explosion which brought down the main wall of the bastion. Hardly had the resultant dust and debris settled down that Piali's troops poured forward and gained a foothold into the town. The bells of the Conventual Church of St Lawrence began to ring the dreaded signal that the enemy had penetrated the fortifications and was in the town.

At that time the grand master was in the clock tower in Birgu's Main Square which served as a command post. He used to control every action from there, but this most urgent situation now required his personal attention. Putting only a light morion on his head, and taking a spike from a soldier, he went down and called his men to follow him. Then he led the way to the bastion of Castile. The presence of the 71-year-old grand master leading a few knights into battle immediately attracted the attention of the townsfolk, and before he knew it de Valette was being followed by the men, women and children of Birgu.

On the first contact with the Turks on the still smouldering slopes of Castile bastion, a grenade exploded very close, and wounded the grand master in the leg. But notwithstanding the shouting of those around him all asking him to withdraw, he kept going and led the crowd into a fierce attack with knights and soldiers using their weapons, and men and women wielding what implements they could find. Where there weren't any, there were ample quantities of stone to be thrown at the enemy. Most surprised were the Turks who in front of this motley force enraged at the investment of their town staggered and withdrew. But limping badly, de Valette continued to lead his people telling them he would not stop so long as the Muslim banners remained on the ramparts. He knew his presence was necessary to inspire all around him to further efforts, and indeed it was only after the Turks were hurled back that he withdrew to have his wound dressed.

The Turks attacked again during the night, starting with ships under Candelissa closing in from Bighi Bay with rippling gunfire which turned the night into day and

Second bombardment on the post of Castille, Birgu, 29 July 1565

making it easier for their land forces to press their action. Somehow the defenders seemed to be containing this onslaught as well. But Mustapha Pasha persisted with this attack as he was now feeling that the defenders could not resist for long.

Jean de Valette felt like this too. His losses had been heavy, and he had no further reinforcements to call upon. Ammunition and supplies had run short, while the hospital was full with the wounded. Those who could stand on their feet had to fight, and many were doing this without any cover since defence posts had been razed to the ground. When the Turks moved their siege engines to climb over still standing bastions teams of Maltese workers were deployed to destroy them. But where knights and soldiers continued to fight from still standing bastions they were now joined by women who began to upturn cauldrons of boiling water on the Turks below. Those who had no place on the bastions attended to feeding and nursing combatants, with children helping in any way they could. A writer of those days described how the tumult of combatants, the sound of arms, the cries of soldiers, with the groans of wounded men and women made a spectacle that was both terrible and moving. What prayers were being said for divine intervention and deliverance were being answered by a miracle of courage.

On 23 August the Council met to consider the situation and there was a proposal to abandon Birgu. It was known that the town was by then honeycombed with the enemy's mines and any further resistance was considered to be dangerous. It was therefore suggested that all should withdraw into Fort St Angelo. But de Valette rejected this suggestion immediately. He said that if Birgu were to be abandoned, Senglea and St Michael would also fall and that would mean the end of Malta, and the Order. There was also the question of the people of Birgu, who could not all be accommodated in Fort St Angelo which was too small, and de Valette continued to say, he was certainly not going to leave any of the loyal Maltese at the mercy of the Turks. If knights, soldiers and Maltese men and women were to die, they would die fighting together.

The other members of the Council had no immediate reply to this exhortation. And in their silence one could sense the deliberations being made. Then as if to emphasize his decision, de Valette said: 'No my brothers, this and this only is the place where we must stand and fight. Here we must all perish together, or finally, with the help of God, succeed in driving off our enemy.'

Then to make sure that his decision would be implemented, the grand master took most of the garrison of St Angelo to Birgu, leaving only enough men to man the guns. And he had the drawbridge which joined the fort to Birgu blown up, so that the town would now be on its own.

If the defenders of Birgu were now desperate, so were the Turks who saw all their efforts being resisted so boldly. The most worried man was however Mustapha Pasha now knowing more than ever before that he could never bring himself to report failure and defeat to the Sultan Suleiman. But rather than finding a way out of his impasse he was now having more difficulties to continue the siege. A ship carrying much needed stores for his army had been captured on its way to Malta by a Sicilian galley, and now he was told that there was only enough flour left for twenty five days. Gunpowder was also running short and he was forced to curtail the rate of firing for his cannons. There was also the question of illness and disease which were still rife amongst his men, and his officers were already reporting having difficulties in controlling them. To make matters even more difficult there was Piali already asking for the withdrawal of the fleet. The time had come for him to employ every stratagem he knew of as a last resort.

There was recourse to other siege engines to be used against the bastions of Castile at Birgu, and it was again the courage of Maltese workmen led by two knights Claramont and Guevarez de Pereira that saved the situation. They opened a way through the bastion wall and charged to capture an engine intact before the Janissaries on the top platform knew what was happening. After sweeping all the Turks from the engine, the Maltese this time did not destroy it so that knights and soldiers could clamber on it with a couple of cannons which they began firing on the attacking Turks.

Not to be outdone Mustapha Pasha ordered his sappers to mine even further beneath the already crumbling bastions of Birgu intending to blow up the whole system of fortifications. Mines were also to be laid further in under parts of the town itself. But again, Maltese workers, this time stonemasons and miners began tunnelling from inside to meet the enemy underground. When they did, there was fighting with pick and shovel. When they did not, mines would very often go off with the falling masonry burying friend and foe.

Much as the defenders persisted in fighting and using their own stratagems to keep the Turks at bay they knew they were at their last gasp, and the end was near. There had already been worked a miracle of courage. But with their bastions breached or demolished, and the remaining knights and other fighting men all wounded or battle weary, there had to be another miracle to prevent their fall.

It could have been that what miraculous intervention they were praying and hoping for on that day came through Mustapha Pasha who as an alternative to give up the siege began considering wintering in Malta. This, he felt, could make it possible for him to recoup his forces and get what supplies he needed for a fresh and later offensive. But to do this he felt he had at least to capture the capital Mdina. This would give him some credit with Suleiman as it would also provide guns and ammunition

The medieval fortified city of Mdina

to be found in the town. So, as if in answer to the defenders' prayers, he stopped the attacks on Birgu and Senglea, and then withdrew his forces to throw them against the capital.

Mdina's garrison was very small, since Don Mesquita the Portuguese Governor of the city had been asked to send most of his best troops to Birgu at the beginning of the siege. On learning of the impending attack on him he knew he was not in a position to resist, so rather than fighting a lost battle he decided to resort to trying to show a bold appearance hoping that desperate as they were the Turks would fall for the bluff. If he didn't have soldiers, he had a lot of peasants and other people who had taken shelter in the city. He took as many as he could from these and had them dressed in soldiers' uniforms. Then he set them to patrol the ramparts. He also concentrated the few cannons he had on the side from which he expected the Turks would appear.

His bluff worked, for when the first enemy troops approached the city they saw a heavily guarded stronghold. Don Mesquita played up by ordering all his cannons to fire some shots even when the enemy was still out of range. So before setting their disgruntled troops on the attack the Turkish officers informed Mustapha Pasha, who fearing another St Elmo gave up his idea and decided to resume his attacks on Birgu and Senglea.

But all this gave the knights a much needed week's respite. And to Jean de Valette the chance to send another message to Don Garcia the viceroy of Sicily as if notwithstanding all the delay and procrastination he had to bear with, he was still inspired that the help he needed would eventually be sent. So much so, that in this which was to be his last message after dwelling on the dire situation in Malta, the grand master went further to tell Don Garcia that he could only land his troops at Mellieħa on the western tip of Malta if he were to avoid being seen by the Turks at Grand Harbour and Marsamxett.

This message was providential. Don Garcia had on the 25 August sailed with 24 galleys and 8,000 men for Malta, but had run into a storm which caused damage to his ships and sickness to his troops. So he had to seek shelter and returned to and returned to Sicily. And that was where he found de Valette's message awaiting him.

8

THE END OF THE SIEGE

Attacks on Birgu and Senglea were resumed on 1 September. But the defenders immediately noticed that what zeal and fire there had always been in the fighting Turks had now all gone out. It seemed as if the strain of three months of fighting was telling on them. This had a salutary effect on the defenders who for the first time began to feel confident of bringing the siege to a successful end which was in sight.

The truth was that Mustapha Pasha did not intend to give up, and further fighting would more likely weaken than strengthen the defenders. The outcome depended more than ever before on whether the Sicilian relief force would arrive in time or not.

The fleet carrying this force was on that day still at still at Sicily where it had reassembled after it had been dispersed by rough weather. There were repairs to be carried out to what was damaged by the storm as many of the soldiers being carried had to get over their bouts of sea sickness. This did not worry the already over sluggish Don Garcia who seemed to welcome the delay in getting involved with the Turks. But with his troops there were also about 200 knights who after having converged on Messina from different parts of Europe in an endeavour to join their brethren in Malta in the fight against the Turks had already made a nuisance of themselves in pressing him for action. Now they became even more scornful of this further delay. Eventually the fleet left Limosa for Malta on 4 September.

Don Garcia did not seem to take the hints given by de Valette in his last message and decided to approach Malta on its western side thus risking being sighted by Turkish ships coming out of Marsamxett. In his history of the Order the Abbe Vertot implies that by this move the viceroy might have been inviting a Turkish intervention and a reason for him to turn back. But whatever was the reason behind Don Garcia's move, the fact remains that, however strange it may seem he was not sighted by the Turks, even if their ships were supposed to be patrolling the Malta channel. It was then on the 6 September that Don Garcia brought his ships round to Mellieħa as suggested in de Valette's message. On the following morning, on the 7th, his 8,000 troops began to land.

Jean de Valette was immediately informed of the arrival of this relief force but when he learned that there were only 8,000 men in it he thought this was not enough to help him oust the Turks. He became worried that Mustapha Pasha would learn this too so on the spur of the moment he had one of his Muslim slaves released telling him to go to his commander-in-chief and tell him that it was no use continuing with the siege now that 16,000 Christian troops had landed in Malta.

The message reached Mustapha Pasha. It also coincided with a decision by Don Garcia who after landing his troops sailed for Sicily but before taking to the open sea made a detour to the south and in front of Grand Harbour in full sight of the Turks all his galleys fired a three gun salute to Fort St Angelo and the Order's flag flying there.

This brought great joy to the Christian garrison. But to Mustapha Pasha it brought disappointment together with a realization that his fleet had been reduced to such a state that it could not challenge the viceroy's ships as they passed by. Added to his other burdens, the arrival of Sicilian reinforcements proved to be the straw that broke the camel's back. And he decided to withdraw from Malta.

Mustafa Pasha (first from left), commander of the army

The bombardments were stopped and all Turkish activity throughout that night was concentrated on dismantling cannons and carrying them back to their ships. On the following day, the 8 of September although the towns of Birgu and Senglea emerged from the morning mist at dawn scathed and pockmarked with battle scars as before, there was no sign of enemy troops. All of them had withdrawn to their ships in Marsamxett and Grand Harbour. Instead of the reverberating sound of cannon and explosions, there could now be heard from Birgu the sweet notes of the bells from the Conventual Church of St Lawrence as they rang over the shattered towns transmitting to all a message of victory. It was on that day also the Feast of the Nativity of the Blessed Virgin to whose intercession the knights and people of Malta believed they owed their deliverance.

Gates were opened and the people could now walk and roam again in freedom as before. But the knights had something else to do. Jean de Valette ordered his respective garrisons to move their cannons to vantage positions from where they soon opened fire on the Turkish fleet that had begun to leave Grand Harbour.

✳   ✳   ✳

When the gunners had fired their last shots at the enemy, they left their place and went to join the other knights, soldiers and Maltese who had assembled in Birgu for the singing of a *Te Deum* in thanksgiving to God. The streets were still littered with used cannon balls, pieces of metal, stone and other war rubble, reflecting all that the people and defenders had been through. But as they moved into the Conventual Church there was soon descending over everyone an aura of silence. Looking over that massed congregation one could not help guessing that during those few moments before the intonement of the *Te Deum* everyone's thoughts must have been of those who could not be there after having paid with the supreme sacrifice of death. But as the thousand voices began chanting the first verses of the hymn of thanksgiving and victory, every man, woman and child that was in the church knew that the sacrifice of their missing brethren had not been in vain.

The departure of the Turkish armada, 13 September 1565

*   *   *

But even so, not everything was over. It was during this ceremony of thanksgiving that guards from St Elmo and Mount Sciberras came quickly to Birgu and informed de Valette that while the Turkish fleet was on its way northwards up the coast, some of the troopships had turned back and were already landing soldiers at Mellieħa and Salina Bays. De Valette could not believe his ears, and asked himself the obvious question. What could have happened?

The answer was that some Turks who had been the last to join their comrades after having been sent to spy on the Sicilian relief force informed Mustapha Pasha of the number of men in that force which was certainly much less that what the commander-in-chief had been led to believe. Indignant at the way he had been fooled Mustapha wanted to take revenge and cancelled his order for evacuation. Admiral Piali disagreed after having been so keen intent to return home. The hostility that had always existed between the two leaders now burst into flames, and also brought a compromise. Mustapha Pasha would land with his troops, and Piali with his fleet would wait for him at St Paul's Bay.

De Valette quickly informed Ascanio de la Corna who was the commander of the Sicilian relief force that the Turks had changed mind and were going to fight. La Coma moved his force to high ground at Naxxar where he intended to wait for the Turks to give battle. But the 200 or so knights who had already forced Don Garcia's hands in Sicily to expedite departure rose up again this time. They had waited for so long to join in the fight, and when they arrived in Malta the Turks had withdrawn. Now that the enemy had come back to give them a chance of a fight, nothing was going to keep them back. And without waiting for La Corna's reaction they spurred down from the ridge towards the oncoming Turks. Some other troops similarly impetuous to get to grips with the enemy followed them. It would have been useless for La Corna to try and hold them back so rather than leaving them alone, outnumbered as they were, he ordered the rest of his troops to follow them as well. The garrison at Mdina had also been following what was happening and on seeing the Sicilian contingents go into action, they did the same intending to take the Turks on their flank.

After more than three months of fighting under the conditions already mentioned, the Turkish troops were certainly no match for the fresh Sicilian force spoiling for a fight. Many Turks broke and ran refusing action, while others halted uncertain what to do. But the knights and the Spanish soldiers making up the force rushed onto the disorganized Turks and a fierce fight ensued. Some of the Turks ran for a tower in the vicinity and made a stronghold out of it, but there was nothing to hold the Spaniards who stormed the place. Seeing that his men were at a disadvantage, Mustapha Pasha himself tried to infuse more courage and determination into his men. When his horse was shot from beneath him, he got on to another one which for the second time was also similarly killed. He could see that his men could not hold the Christians and had to consent when they began to retreat. So he put his Janissary arquebusiers at the front in an attempt to hold the Christians at bay while his other troops could retreat to St Paul's Bay and embark on the boats awaiting them there. But even so, the knights and Spanish troops broke through the Janissaries and followed the Turks right to the shore of St Paul's Bay fighting with axe and sword, and even going into the sea where they could upturn their boats.

Mustapha Pasha had never seen anything like this and he realized his blunder in having come back. When he had his troops back on their ships, and still under a rattle of fire from the Spanish musketeers he had to leave three thousand dead behind him, scattered all along the roads and ridges where the battle had taken place, with a few hundred bodies floating in the bay as if to press home the extent of his defeat. The humbled Turkish armada left for Costantinople by the evening of 14 September 1565. The Siege of Malta had ended.

*　　　　　*　　　　　*

All Europe rejoiced at the Maltese victory over the Turks. Bells rang in churches from Palermo to Paris and even in London where the Archbishop of Canterbury Matthew Parker laid down a Form of Thanksgiving for six weeks. The island was now dubbed as 'The Island of Heroes' and *The Bulwark of the Faith*. Honours were bestowed upon Grand Master de Valette. Philip II of Spain sent him a jewelled sword and poniard of enamelled gold set with pearls and diamonds. Pope Pius V sent the grand master a cardinal's hat which Jean de Valette declined since his time was all taken up by his duties as a grand master of the Order. But then he was already enjoying a cardinal's distinction without any involvement with the Vatican.

The Church now planned that it would henceforth commemorate the occasion by a Pontifical high mass to be sung in thanksgiving on 8 September of each year. The knights laid down a regatta to be held in Grand Harbour on the same date. Both these commemorative functions continued to be held till these very days. In recognition of their part in the Siege, the town of Senglea was to be called 'Invicta' meaning Unconquered, while Birgu was renamed Vittoriosa, meaning 'the Victorious City' by which names both towns are still known today. Nonetheless both of them then presented a very desolate outlook with their ramparts razed to the ground and their residential areas demolished. Burnt out villages and empty water cisterns added to the grim picture and the outlook brought forth some suggestions to have the knights abandon Malta and go back to Sicily.

But de Valette would not hear of this. Fired by the glory and success attained he was ready to bury himself beneath Malta's ruins rather than abandon the island. And he was not alone in this belief since there were others who like him felt that the Great Siege had settled once and for all the question of the Order's home. The knights had not been able to stay in Palestine, as they had also had to leave Cyprus, and to be eventually also ousted from Rhodes. Their victory against the Turks at Malta had earned them the right to make the island their permanent home. Then one could not lose sight of the fact that with her strategic position, astride the trade routes of the Mediterranean, Malta could offer more to the Order in its commerce and its sworn fight against Islam.

It was the time for the Order to

The Great Siege graveyard monument in the grounds of St John co-cathedral change its title, and become the Sovereign Military and Hospitaller Order of St John of Jerusalem, Rhodes and Malta. Its members were henceforth to be known as the knights of Malta.

Valletta with its parallel streets leading to Fort St Elmo
Inset: Mount Sciberras at the time of the Great Siege

9

TIMES OF PROGRESS AND TURBULENCE

Jean de Valette had indeed become the toast of Christian Europe. But nonetheless he did not allow this to go to his head. His most immediate commitment was to repair the defences that had been razed to the ground; and this was pressing upon him because he believed that the Turks would very likely launch another attack on Malta. But even so, now that it had been established that Malta was to remain the home and headquarters of the Order of St John, the caring grand master was dead intent on building a city which would be worthy of the future he could foresee for the Order and its projected city he chose Mount Sciberras.

Francesco Laparelli (1521–70)
soldier and military expert

and its knights. As a site for this projected city he chose Mount Sciberras.

It must be said that a suggestion of this sort had already been made by Count Strozzi who had first suggested the building of Fort St Elmo, and by Antonio Ferramolino who had redesigned Fort St Angelo and the defences of Birgu, now called Vittoriosa. But this does not detract from de Valette's efforts. The two mentioned gentlemen had only expressed an idea, but it was de Valette who threw himself heart and soul into the matter to make the dream come true. The biggest problem that assailed him was the lacking finances. But encouraged by the high esteem he was then enjoying he appealed for help and sent his ambassadors to the sovereigns of Christendom. Response was good. The King of France sent him 140,000 livres, while Philip II of Spain was willing to fork out another 90,000. The King of Portugal promised him 90,000 crusadoes, and the Pope sent him 15,000 crowns. With his donation then, on 28 December 1565, the Pontiff also sent the Italian engineer Francesco Laparelli with the plans both for the new defences and the city that was to be built.

There was also substantial contributions made by the commanders and knights of the Order who could afford them from their private means. But there were also those amongst them who could not afford liquid cash, and readily sold their furniture and private effects to raise the donation they wanted to make.

No time was lost and after the lines were marked out for the city and its fortifications, the foundation stone was laid down on 28 March 1566. It was a great occasion for the grand master with his council and knights who met on those memorable slopes on that morning in spring to inaugurate the splendid city that was to bear his name. The foundation stone was appropriately engraved in Latin with the following inscription:-

'The most illustrious and most reverend Lord, Brother de Valette, grand master of the Order of St John of Jerusalem, both hospitaller and military, considering all the perils to which his knights and the people of Malta had been exposed during the last siege by the infidels; and having with the approbation of the council of the Order, and for the better opposition of new attacks from the barbarians, resolved to build a

Our Lady of Victory Church, Valletta

70

city upon Mount Sciberras; the said grand master had this day, being Thursday, the twenty-eighth of March of the present year 1566 (after having called upon the holy name of God, and besought the intercession of the Holy Virgin his mother, and of St John the Baptist, titular patron of the Order, to obtain the blessing of heaven upon this important work) laid the first stone of it with his arms, which are a *leon d'or* in a field gules engraved upon it; and the new city by his order has been named the city of La Valette.'

Beneath the stone there were thrown gold and silver medals with the inscription in Latin Melita Renascence meaning the rebirth of Malta.

Every member of the Order was detailed to contribute his share in the building. There were the knights who with their galleys were engaged on the bringing of materials from Sicily and Italy; others went even as far as Lyons in France to bring new artillery castings. Most of the rest then had to supervise the groups of workers that were engaged on the actual building, and there were 8,000 of these. Even the grand master himself began spending whole days on the building sites, very often also having his meals there as if not wanting to let out of his sight the sprouting city of his dreams.

The first building that was to be constructed was a chapel dedicated to Our Lady of Victories where de Valette decreed he wanted to be buried after his death.

Notwithstanding the care and attention being given there were problems. One of these concerned the lack of money to pay wages whenever foreign contributions did not arrive in time. The grand master solved this by casting new brass coins showing on one side two hands joined together and on the other side his arms quartered with those of the Order, with the Latin wording *Non aes sed fides*, meaning 'not cash but credit'. These coins were paid to the workers in the way of an IOU when there was no money. They could then be exchanged for cash when this became available later. The system worked and there was no slackness in the building of the city.

Another problem that assailed de Valette was the fear of another Turkish attack and siege which he knew he was not in a position to resist if it were to materialize. The situation might have tended to become more pressing when the galleys of the Order were refitted and re-equipped and began to be sent out to raid the Turkish supply lines. An immediate remedy was sought by persuading Philip II of Spain to send 15,000 soldiers to garrison the island until the defences were reinstated. When these arrived everyone was relieved, and there were those who might have thought de Valette to have been over-cautious.

But in fact he was not, and the likelihood of another attack by the Turks was no fluke. Furious after the defeat of his armada, Sultan Suleiman had decided on another attack on Malta which he wanted to lead himself. And it was in the middle of 1566 with the building of Valletta in full swing that de Valette was informed by his spies of the increased activities at the Turkish arsenal in Istanbul. New galleys and galleots were being built, with the obvious scope of mounting the dreaded attack. Jean de Valette realized that by the time such an attack would be launched he would not have completed his defences. So rather than waiting longer in suspense he took the bull by the horns, and arranged with his spies in Istanbul to set the arsenal on fire, which they did, blowing up magazines and destroying most of the galleys and galleots that were being constructed there. Because of this setback Suleiman 'decided to postpone his intended attack on Malta and turned his attention to the war in Hungary. But while leading the siege of Szigetvar himself, he died on 5 September 1566. His son Selimur who succeeded him was not that keen on attacking Malta, and turned his attention against Venice.

While this was a relief for de Valette, it also raised another problem with the building of Valletta. The configuration of the site of Mount Sciberras had from the start required a lot of levelling before the city could be built as the designers intended. But with the scare of another Turkish attack all levelling was stopped so as to devote more time and work on fortifications. Now that the scare was over the lack of levelling could only be remedied by constructing streets of steps where the land sloped sharply down to the sea. One such spot affected by this remedy was that which came to be known as the Manderaggio. The name devolves from Mandraki a word which described smaller craft used by the knights at Rhodes and for which they provided a small harbour behind or adjacent to Grand Harbour. Mandraki is in fact the diminutive of the Greek word *mandra*, meaning a sheep-fold, hence applied to the berthing place of small ships. The Manderaggio at Valletta was for centuries inhabited by boatmen and watermen who were perhaps poor, and was therefore considered as a slum area which has of course changed by time.

However one bigger problem which began to preoccupy de Valette at this time concerned his young knights. Apart from serious doubts about the keeping of their vows, there were more often cases of insubordination. It seems as if some upstarts were already envisaging a new face for the Order which of course de Valette being a strict disciplinarian could not tolerate. The situation came into the open when a band of knights, mostly Spanish became drunk and disorderly and began singing songs they had composed themselves which mocked other senior knights and also the honour of some principal ladies of Malta. An indignant de Valette referred the matter to the council which decided on taking disciplinary action. But whilst the council was still in session and the vice-chancellor was writing the sentence to be meted out, the rebellious knights entered the chamber in force, took the pen from the vice-chancellor's hand and threw it out of the window. They then had to be thrown out of the chamber by force. From there they went straight to the harbour where they had commandeered a felucca and sailed away to Sicily. More than a prank by young drunken upstarts the grand master considered this as a mutinous act. He sent one of his senior knights Chevalier Caprona to the viceroy of Sicily and demanded the capture of these knights who were to be returned to Malta where they would be unfrocked and sent to life imprisonment. But they were never found, and had most probably returned to their respective countries. Jean de Valette took this matter so badly that it affected his health. More than a mere escapade he saw in it a red light for the future of his knights, in the wake of the waves of Reformation that were already being felt in some countries of Europe.

This deterioration in behaviour of the knights was now contrasted with better relations between the Maltese people and the Order. Maybe because of their valid cooperation during the Great Siege, the Maltese could now aspire to even higher appointments with the Order. Some acquired officer status at important establishments like the Treasury, others became Lawyers, Jurymen and Magistrates. Even if such a transformation began to take place from middle classes, those in the upper class began to thaw. And there were even the aspirations for members of such families to join the Order, which however they could not do. This was because mindful of the Templars, the knights remained very sensitive to any suggestion of a 'Saracen' taint. And they suspected that the old Maltese nobility had intermarried with peasant stock of the Muslim population. They therefore continued to refuse, no matter how splendid the family blazon, to admit gentlemen of Maltese birth to the Order.

When in July 1568 the grand master succumbed to sunstroke after a day's hawking in the strong Malta sun he knew the end was near. It was expected that he would make his last dispositions, but much as there was to be done, he paid more attention to arranging for his household slaves to be set at liberty, and to forgive his enemies. He also granted a pardon to the group of knights who had rebelled and escaped, and made provisions for their acceptance back into the Order should they ever return. The rest of his days he devoted to appealing to his knights to live together in peace and unity, and to uphold the ideals of the Order he had served so faithfully. On 21 August 1568 he died, and was according to his wishes laid to rest in the chapel built in Valletta dedicated to the Blessed Virgin, Our Lady of Victory. His demise brought to an end one of the most illustrious epochs of the knights of Malta, and this became evident on the faces and behaviour of the silent crowds that participated in his funeral along the streets of Vittoriosa and then across the harbour to the city that bore his name.

*   *   *

Being already 71, the new grand master, an Italian Pietro del Monte could not be expected to take the same firm control of the young unruly knights as his predecessor had done. But it seems that he threw himself heart and soul into continuing with the building of Valletta. It was he who now started to build the first houses, and it is not excluded that behind this there might have been the intention to retain the good relations de Valette had begun to establish with the population. There was a similar move made with the intention to take better control of the knights when he began planning to start building the Auberges of the various Langues. These had to be majestic buildings and were entrusted for construction to the renowned Maltese architect Gerolamo Cassar who had done the fortifications. The original idea was to reproduce the Rhodian system whereby the knights would live in a conventual enclosure

Gerolamo Cassar (1520–92)

73

The Auberge of Castille, Leon and Portugal, Valletta

called the Collachium, and which would be separated by a wall from the burgh of the general public, but this was found to be impracticable. So it was agreed that the new Auberges would not offer cloistered seclusion and they would be scattered side by side with houses for the population. But nonetheless the knights would henceforth have to stick to their proper system of living in the new buildings, something they could not do in their small habitations in Vittoriosa.

The system envisaged that the Auberges would be presided over by the head of the Langue, who bore the title of pilier. As such he was also one of the principal dignitaries of the Convent, with the pillar of each Langue having also a special charge at headquarters. So much so that the pillar of France was the Grand Hospitaller, while the pillar of Provence was the grand preceptor of the Order of the Order and supervised the Treasury. The pillars of Italy and Castile were grand admiral and grand chancellor respectively while the pillar of England bore the title of Turcopolier. Within the Auberge the pillar had to exercise discipline over the knights of his Langue and he presided at all meals at a separate table. He was to be seated on a raised platform with the privilege of a carpet and a cushion for his feet. The young knights sat on benches covered only with cloth which in the case of grand crosses was replaced by velvet. Below the knights would sit the Chaplains and the Servants-At-Arms. Every knight was obliged to dine at the Auberge at least four times a week while no women or dogs were at any time allowed into the Auberge.

There was an exception in the case of *Commandeurs* controlling a commandery. The Order's commanderies, all over Europe which linked it with feudal nobility were very rich properties. So in attaining control of such a commandery, the commander was expected to maintain a separate establishment and more of an independent enclave. There were several of such establishments to be built in Malta, all of them magnificent palaces bearing the name of the *Commandeur* that built them and which were eventually to become familiar landmarks in the history of the knights of Malta. Carafa, Parisio, De la Salle, Verdelin, Bichi (eventually changed to Bighi by usage), Spinola, Vilhena, Cotoner and Scaglia were only a few of them, to be found in this work later on. A very particular one then was Demandolx, whose magnificent city palace is still standing in South Street.

There is no doubt however that notwithstanding such activities, a sense of apathy and inertia had crept in the military side of the Order. It is true that with the fortifications almost completed and the presence of the 15,000 strong Spanish garrison the grand master and his knights could afford to leave military matters aside, but it was not the same where the navy was concerned. Particularly at that time when the forces of Islam were lifting their heads again, and their navy was plying the Mediterranean in force. Del Monte must have been shaken up from his lethargy when in 1570 one of his captains, General Francesco St Clement with four ill-found and undermanned galleys, was put to ignominious flight by a flotilla of the renegade corsair Luciali off the Tunisian coast. On his return to Malta, St Clement was court-martialed and found guilty of cowardice in face of the enemy, and was sentenced to be strangled and flung over the bastions into the sea. It was a ferocious piece of discipline, but it must have paid dividends in having the grand master see to the preparedness of his fleet in time for the Battle of Lepanto a year later on 9 October 1571. On that occasion the Order's galleys under the redoubtable Chevalier Romegas who was the finest seaman the Order had ever produced, together with an Italian squadron under Andrea Doria, both under the command of Don John of Austria, met the Ottoman fleet at Lepanto. A battle was fought, and one of the Turkish commanders who was none other than El Louck, Governor of Alexandria who had taken part in the Great Siege of Malta completely out manoeuvred Andrea Doria and drove in the right wing of the Christian fleet. But Romegas pressed hard on his own on the Turkish centre under its commander-in-chief Aly Pasha and routed the rest of his fleet. El Louck escaped with his ships, but the fleet and force of Islam was destroyed.

There is no doubt that this exploit did much to reassert the Order's prowess and name in Europe. The Battle of Lepanto went down in history as the turning point in establishing the prestige and striking power of the Order's navy. The knights were soon to be recognized as the policemen of the Mediterranean, setting free Christian captives and seeking out pirates and corsairs and taking even more slaves as hostages to be ransomed for gold to swell the Order's coffers thus contributing directly to its progress in Malta. The strategic crux of the Western world however was at the time to be no longer where it had been before, and with Turkish eyes now turning eastwards the naval war in the Mediterranean tended to die away. This started a new war which nobody announced, and which Western nations entered with open eyes to fight in the Atlantic beyond the pillars of Hercules. It was a war by Protestant England and later Holland to wrest the mastery of the seas from the Catholic king of Spain. At the same time leaving the Order to rest on its laurels and concentrate on internal affairs.

And Pietro del Monte did just that. His first reaction was to transfer the Convent (as the central body of the Order was called) from Vittoriosa to Valletta, now that the building of the city had progressed enough for this. He even went to the extreme of making shift for a while with wooden quarters for himself until he could move to a proper house built by his nephew. With the Order's peace of mind now restored work on the city gathered momentum and by the following year there were completed about two thousand houses which gave the city the first look of the homogenous Renaissance town it was intended to be. The knights now began to refer to Mdina (or Notabile) as Città Vecchia, 'the old city', to distinguish it from their new city of Valletta.

This new state of dignity acquired by the Order continued to make itself felt all over Europe where more than ever before admission to the brotherhood was being considered as a privilege. This attracted more noblemen and other gentlemen. And these brought with them the first seeds of the Reformation already prevalent in countries of Europe. This added another challenge to the grand master over his other one of carrying out his more important task of attending to internal affairs, in particular the improvement of relations with the Maltese. But much as he must have been willing to take this, Pietro del Monte died in 1572, and bequeathed his problems to his successor whose reign was to have a very profound effect on the future of the knights of Malta.

Chevalier Jean l'Eveque de la Cassiere, a French knight, was the grand marshal of the Order. For 40 years he had been an honest soldier, and had started his military service with the ill-starred expedition to Modan in 1531 under Salviati, then grand prior of Rome. He had his second blooding with the galleys in an attack on Tunis under Admiral Andrea Doria when driving away Barbarossa from that part of Africa. After that he also took part in the ill-fated attack on Zwara, where however he distinguished himself by saving the Order's Standard. Other than this military aptitude, and his great zeal for the Order he did not have any other qualities to make him aspire to be considered for election to grand master after the death of Pietro del Monte.

In fact the knights had proposed Bali de Montgaudin, the Treasurer of the Order for the post, and Ventemille, the powerful grand prior of Toulouse. But both contestants polled the same number of votes and notwithstanding six hours of battling and voting, the position did not change and it became obvious to all that the elections had run into a deadlock. So in a way of a compromise it was agreed that both contestants would withdraw, and Jean l'Eveque de la Cassiere was elected as the new grand master.

It could have been that many of the knights had chosen him because knowing of his lack of experience of ecclesiastical subtleties and ambitions as well as the lack of any understanding of the ulterior motives in men's hearts he would be lax and easy to be cajoled into their new way of life. Indeed they might even have been misled to believe in their right selection when sparked by his great determination to hold up the standards of the Order as they had been inherited from L'Isle-Adam and de Valette, La Cassiere began to build St John's co-cathedral in Valletta on the plans of the Maltese architect Gerolamo Cassar.

He could foresee that the Order merited something bigger and more imposing, as indeed St John's was eventually to become the Valhalla of the knights.

But there was general disagreement to this move amongst the knights. The majority thought that their grand master had dissipated the patrimony of the Order by building St John's Church, rather than providing magazines to store necessary food stuffs.

But even in a relatively short time after his election the grand master could not help realizing that there was a growing indifference amongst the knights to the preservation of old monastic traditions, with discipline in the Convent becoming lax. Behaviour in Auberges had distinctly deteriorated and he came to know of instances when the knights beat their servants and also broke the rule of Quarantine. He attributed this deterioration to the waves of Reformation which had already begun to threaten the Ordinal Priorities and could also have reached the threshold of his own. He was no fool. But he was obstinate. And once he had a fixation nothing would remove it. Fortunately enough his first whim now was that with the abating of warlike commitments the knights had little if any more to do that fell within the purposes for which the Order had come into being, and this prompted him to start building the Sacred Infirmary in Valletta. This was a hospital intended to make the knights practice their role of hospitallers. It was eventually to become the most celebrated institution of its kind in the Western world. Not only in size, with its main hall being 502 feet in length and 34½ feet in width, but also in service.

This hospital was placed under the jurisdiction of the French Langue but each of the other Langues was allotted one day every week, with the respective members of the Order including novices having to wait on the sick. The grand master himself made it a point to go to the hospital on Fridays. Besides having the benefit of experienced medical, surgical and nursing staff, the patients were fed well, and it is said that two hundred fowls were used daily for chicken broth. Meals were served in silver plates, and the hospital catered for all types of patients including slaves. Indeed there were occasions when patients from foreign countries of Europe having no connection with the Order began to come to Malta for treatment at the hospital.

Much as this was another feather in his cap, La Cassiere continued to be assailed with other problems. In fact it was in 1574 and the year when he started building the hospital that there were news of the Grand Seignor Selimus II, a descendant of Suleiman the Magnificent who was believed to be preparing another attack on Malta. La Cassiere and his knights were caught unprepared and it was fortunate for them that Selimus finished by attacking Tunis. But the harm was done, and the grand master was eventually reproached for having made no provisions against any Turkish attack which might have prejudiced the existence of the Order. But what hurt La Cassiere most was the fact that most of his knights took the opposite side in the matter. Indeed they said that their grand master was more preoccupied with their misconduct with women than with the state of defence. Nonetheless when some of these same knights seized merchandise belonging to some Jews while it was being carried in a Venetian vessel, and a dispute arose with the republic of Venice, La Cassiere took his knights' side pleading that as the Jews were not subjects of the republic the capture of the booty was justified although it was being carried in a friendly vessel. This matter was eventually referred to Rome where it was decided that the booty had to be returned to the Jews. And the Pope's decision was always final, even if it dealt with the most minor of matters. It was at about this time that the Pontiff sent a Chevalier de Mendoza to La Cassiere with instructions to have him take the vows and then to be made grand cross and Turcopolier of the Langue of England which was being revived. It goes however to the grand master's credit that even such irregular acts from those above him did not make him budge an inch from what he considered to be the proper administration of justice even in face of antagonism from his knights. When there were abuses of maladministration of certain services in the commanderie of Germany, he promptly appointed Brother George de Schorbon to investigate and redress. When a Portuguese Knight Chevalier Correa was murdered by six other knights of the same Langue, he quickly had them arrested and tried. When found guilty he had them sentenced to be sewed up in sacks and thrown into the sea. The knights might have said this was the time when their grand master was at his worst. But the truth is that he was at his best. Only that he was tactless, and obstinate even when he might have taken the wrong decision.

La Cassiere might even have regained some of his lost popularity when the building of St John's Church, a still recognized feat in the annals of the Order, was completed in 1578. The church was consecrated on 20 February of that year by Monsignor Ludovico de Torres, Archbishop of Monreale (Sicily) duly authorized by a Papal Brief of Pope Gregory XIII.

He could have enlisted Maltese sympathy by making a case for acceptance of Maltese nobles in the Order. But he did not hesitate to stick to the Order's views about it. This came at a time when some of them had for years been helping in the administration of the island by sitting on the autonomous Commune 'Università'. Others had thawed in their original stiff attitude towards the knights. One of them had now even generously provided the land on which La Cassiere was to build his third monumental edifice, the palace of the grand masters in Valletta; with the perpetual leasehold being a nominal annual giving of five grains of wheat, and the offering of a glass of water from the palace well by the grand master to the head of the family.

Such attitude might have even made the people sympathize with the knights in their silent fight against their grand master. There were now more cases of knights leaving their Auberge without permission, or fighting soldiers of the Order at Vittoriosa very often because of trivialities. On one occasion knights were caught taking cargo from a captured galley after this was towed in port. There were also cases of open acts of disrespect towards La Cassiere. In one instance it was a Bali who after hearing his grand master say what type of baldachin he wanted, told him that he could not have it because his predecessor never had one like it. The incident was closed after the Bali was made to apologize. But La Cassiere knew that things were going out of hand, and he could foresee a rebellion by his knights. His obsession with the evils of Reformation then made him commit his biggest error when attributing what was happening to the 'pestilential heresies' of this Reformation he introduced the Inquisition in Malta. It was a decision which he had reason to regret throughout the rest of his life. But it was also what took the flame to the powder keg.

The rebel knights now concluded that the grand master was too old and not competent to rule any longer. Then under the leadership of none other than Chevalier Romegas the renowned naval commander and whom La Cassiere had promoted to general of the galleys, they took matters into their own hands. They impeached the grand master and forcibly removed him to a prison at Fort St Angelo. Then they elected Romegas as lieutenant grand master to take over.

The case had to be heard in Rome, and although now an octogenerian and broken down by fatigue La Cassiere had to go to Rome with his accusers. The voyage was too much for him, but maybe because his obstinacy this once came to his help, he made it, and was declared innocent. It was then the turn for Romegas to be called to Rome and ask pardon of his superior whom he had helped to unseat and had grievously wronged. But Romegas took this matter so badly that he died of chagrin before he could repair the damage he had done.

True till the end to his Christian principles, La Cassiere forgave Romegas and also asked the knights then in Rome to attend the rebel's funeral and pray for his soul. Then with his conscience at ease he died in December 1581 before he could return to Malta and to his throne. It was only his heart that was buried in Rome. His body was returned for burial in Malta, the land he loved so much. He was buried in the crypt of St John's, where the remains of the previous grand masters had already been transferred in 1577 from the crypt beneath the church dedicated to *St Anne* in Fort St Angelo where they had been buried until then. St John's Church had by now become the Conventual Church of the Order instead of that of St Lawrence, which was returned as the Parish Church of Vittoriosa.

St John co-cathedral, built in 1573 by Grand Master La Cassiere

10

THE INQUISITION

The Holy Inquisition was an old institution for rooting out heresy. It was sparked in its simplest and harmless form by the Society of Jesus founded in 1540 by a Spanish Knight Ignatius Loyola who wanted to combat heresy. It was later furbished by the Council of Trent (1545–63) which abolished most of the evils attacked by Luther and defined the essential doctrines of the church, but eventually became a system of

The Inquisitor's Palace, Vittoriosa

The marble tombs which make up the floor of St John co-cathedral

secret police and tribunals. It was encouraged by King Philip II of Spain who although was then the most powerful monarch in the world found out that Queen Elizabeth of England could or would not do anything to stop raids by English buccaneers on Spanish ports and shipping when their countries were not at war. Using the Inquisition to torture and kill all of the Englishmen that were captured served the purpose in his self-appointed task to destroy Protestantism.

Even though Grand Master Jean d'Eveque de la Cassiere had gone down in the annals of history as the one who had also introduced the Inquisition to Malta and the Order, there are certain facts which must be made clear. It must be said that the first attempts to introduce inquisition in Malta had already been made in the

81

Medieval period. This was a token one, as there do not seem to have been any great upheavals because of it. In 1559 there was another attempt to introduce a more permanent Inquisition in Malta, when de Valette was grand master. On that occasion the Holy See in Rome when Pope Pius IV had assembled the Council of Trent with the purposes already mentioned, wanted to send an Inquisitor to Malta to enquire into the conduct of the knights who may be suspected of heresy. But de Valette was quick to react and sent Knight Commander Francesco la Motta to plead with the Pope, then Pius IV, that this was not necessary as the knights had always kept intact their Catholic faith. Two years later, on 21 October 1561 the Holy See wrote again, this time to the Bishop of Malta, then Monsignor Domenico Cubelles, and to the prior of the Order's Conventual Church as well as to the vice-chancellor of the Order, saying that since there was no Inquisition in Malta, they were authorized to act as Inquisitor in cases of suspected heresy.

This indicates most clearly that the first ideas about the Inquisition did not really come from La Cassiere. Even so, although he had decided to introduce it, it seems that he had never asked for it. According to a writer Del Pozzo, what was interpreted to have been an official request by the grand master to Rome for the introduction of Inquisition was nothing of the sort. La Cassiere had indeed sent Knight Giorgio Vercelli to see the Pope in Rome at the time, but his assignment did not concern the Inquisition. His brief is said to have been threefold; firstly to ask for the confirmation of all privileges and statutes of the Order; secondly he was to ask for the right to impose tax on the Bishop's revenue, until that time being paid to the viceroy of Sicily; and thirdly he was to ask for a special concession to be given to the prior of the Conventual Church to erect and bless burial places in the new city of Valletta. This last request was intended to start burying grand masters at the then completed St John's Church.

It so happened that by the time Vercelli reached Rome, Pope Pius V died, and the request had to be made to his successor Pope Gregory XIII who was required as well to appoint a new Bishop of Malta since the post had become vacant. And against the recommendations of the grand master, the Pontiff appointed the vice-chancellor of the Order Roias as Bishop. It could be that because he knew that his appointment was not approved by La Cassiere, Roias might have influenced the Pope with his resulting brief of 20 April 1573 which besides appointing him Bishop also empowered him to inquire into all cases of heresy by members of religious orders including the knights.

However, notwithstanding his preoccupation with the knights' behaviour La Cassiere reacted strongly to this and sent Knight Cosimo de Luna to Rome with the assignment to ask the Pope to revoke the special powers given to the Bishop. The Pope took his time to consider this, but eventually agreed to do so, however with the proviso that he would send an Apostolic Delegate to Malta, besides the Bishop, to act as Inquisitor. This time La Cassiere could not object, and on 1 August 1574 welcomed Monsignor Peter Dusina as the first Inquisitor general for Malta. He provided him with a residence at Valletta, but he was to hold court in Fort St Elmo.

One of the Inquisitor's first acts was to establish a Tribunal of the Inquisition which meant the bestowal on special judges, powers in matters of faith by the supreme ecclesiastical authority. The Tribunal had to deal legally with offences against the

Faith, and also to pronounce judgment according to statutes of canonical procedure and impose penalties. Concurrently with this the faithful were asked and indeed' encouraged to give information on local heretics. The outcome was that very few, if any, of the faithful went forward with information, while many not so faithful discovered an easy way of taking vengeance on those they hated by reporting them for heresy. And a mere allegation or suspicion was enough for the Inquisitor to judge and mete out punishment.

It was not long when everyone disliked the Inquisitor. If the knights had always looked at the Bishop as the agent of the King, they now began to look at the Inquisitor as the spy of the Pope, and they had to be on their guard since the Inquisitor as had already been said could punish on a mere accusation without waiting for any proof. So while they had on more than one occasion resented the intrusion of the Bishop into the Religion and even refused him the right to vote, it was going to be difficult going in the case of the Inquisitor. It can be said that there was also no love lost between the Inquisitor and the Bishop, and both of them lost no time in setting up their own particular empires. The former filling his dungeons with alleged heretics, and the latter by removing persons from the jurisdiction of the Order by turning them into 'clerks' complete with tonsure and imposed, however unwanted, celibacy.

Even though the grand master and the Inquisitor showed a courteous front to each other there were soon sprouting antagonistic feelings towards each other with both of them doing their utmost to concede the absolute minimum of deference. Protocol demanded that when a new Inquisitor went for his first audience to the

Prisoner's cells at the Inquisitor's Palace, Vittoriosa

grand master's palace, on his arrival at the first ante-chamber the curtain between it and the next room was to be drawn apart. But since no such compliment was paid to grand crosses of the Order, the curtain on such occasions began to be merely raised by a chamberlain so as not to show greater deference than that shown to members of the Order. Protocol also laid down that on meeting the grand master the Inquisitor was to be lead by him into the audience chamber where he would then be asked to be seated. At the end of the audience then he would make the first move without waiting for any sign. He would then be accompanied by the grand master only to the second chamber from where he would then be conducted by a senior chamberlain to the top of the staircase, and from there by chamberlains of lower rank to the bottom of the stairs.

There was also protocol to be observed when the grand master and the Inquisitor met in the street. If they happened to be both in their coaches, then the Inquisitor was to stop and allow the grand master's coach to pass, but if he happens to be in his coach and the grand master is on foot, then the Inquisitor should descend from his coach and pay his compliment to the grand master, who was also obliged to stop and acknowledge the compliment. If on the other hand the grand master was in his coach and the Inquisitor on foot, then the latter would be expected to make a profound salute and continues on his way without accosting the coach.

The Inquisitor's Palace Courtyard, Vittoriosa

One of the grand master's distasteful obligations was to invite the Inquisitor to dinner three times a year, at Carnival, Easter and Christmas. From his end the Inquisitor was compelled to call on the grand master to give him Christmas greetings. These were all small things, but nonetheless annoying. And they had to be carried out even if as it was obvious to all, they did not carry the sense of respect that was intended to be behind them. After all the grand master could not afford to offend the Pope, and the Inquisitor dared not face the loss of prestige by failing in his duties.

La Cassiere had to face all this for seven years in confrontation with four Inquisitors, since these had a term of office of two years. He had only a slight respite before being offered the old Castellania palace in Birgu as his new resident and office. The palace was to be found in Vittoriosa, and moved out of Valletta. Rising tall and grim among the narrow streets of the city, this sunless building, complete with torture chambers, small cells and exercise yards, leave a harsh reminder of the Inquisition until these very days.

The post of Inquisitor to Malta was considered to be a very important one, and was always filled by persons of distinction. Of the sixty nine inquisitors accredited to the Order in Malta, twenty five were subsequently elected Cardinals of the Church, while two ultimately became Popes as Alexander VII and Innocent XII.

It was to be expected that the knights were not likely to clash with the Inquisition because of heresy. However it did not take long to be noticed that there were other circumstances more than heresy to make an inquisitor pounce. In fact we have it that pretty soon after Dusina, the first inquisitor had shed off his sheep's skin it became common knowledge that beside suspicion and hostility, the inquisition was also responsible for keeping a querulous watch for impertinences from knights, and any systematic encouragement of jealousies and dissensions in the order which might tend to weaken authority of the grand master.

When Knight Chevalier Charles Valdina lost his temper and attacked the Inquisitor's secretary at the old Infirmary in Vittoriosa, the Inquisitor himself thought that the matter was so straightforward that he proceeded to give judgment without any reference to the Tribunal. But rather than staying back to watch justice being done by the Inquisitor the knights rose up like one and protested to Rome on behalf of their comrade saying the Inquisitor was not within his right to judge without the assistance of the Tribunal. But the Pontiff found for the Inquisitor, and Valdina was exiled from Malta for one year. There was another occasion when the Inquisitor's jurisdiction was questioned. This time it was Inquisitor Monsignor Antonio Ortensio who wanted to stop the departure of the captain of a French galley to Marseilles because he was accused of a heretical proposition. So the captain was arrested and put into prison to await trial. However, some French knights freed their compatriot captain and taking him to his galley still in harbour they tried to help him escape. Knowing that they had been recognized they were also leaving as well. But the Order's galleys in harbour were, at the request of the Inquisitor, ordered to open fire on the escaping galley which was in fact stopped, with the captain and the knights being apprehended and eventually put on trial.

These and many other similar incidents indicate that after all the knights were not that much intimidated by the Inquisitor and did not always take his ways lying down. Rather than looking to their grand master when thinking they were in the right, they would appeal straight to the Pope; when they weren't or were in doubt, they took matters into their own hands. There was a case when Knight Chevalier Pontoise attacked and injured a labourer employed with the Inquisitor. The Bishop's Vicar, at the time Monsignor Fabrizi, tried to take action against Pontoise. But other knights intervened and in the process took hold of Monsignor Fabrizi and tried to throw him over the bastions of Valletta. But perhaps one of the worst reactions by the knights against the Inquisition came in the time of Inquisitor Monsignor Louis

Serridori when he forced the grand master of the time to imprison Knight Chevalier Jerome de Galian Caster Nuovo, and this because of a heated discussion with the Procurator Fiscal of the Inquisition Paul Testaferrata, a Maltese, about the religion embraced by an Ethopian slave-girl. Knights went on a rampage and they first broke down doors at Fort St Angelo and then again at Fort St Elmo until they found their colleague and set him free.

There were of course cases when the grand master himself would take a matter in his own hands. When for example Knight Chevalier Charles of Aymede murdered Dr Frederick Ciantar, a Maltese and Notary of the Inquisition, the grand master appealed to the Pope and asked for a brief to mitigate the Inquisitor's powers in this case. But the Pontiff had in this case ordered the Tribunal to proceed and Aymede was found guilty and deprived of the habit to be subsequently hanged in the courtyard of the Inquisitor's palace.

What might have appeared strange was how and why the Pope would very often seem to welcome the knights appealing or going to him with complaints about the grand master or the Inquisitor. The answer is that through such interventions the Pontiff was always gaining more information about the members of the Order which was thus never away from the closest surveillance of Rome through the Inquisition. And this sometimes made the Pope supervise and even manipulate the election of some grand master.

What became evident was that the Inquisitor seems to have become no match for grand masters who were made Cardinal Princes, and their clashes, when they occurred, concerned acrimonious disputes largely on matters of jurisdiction and precedence.

11

A PRINCE AMONGST PAUPERS

Hugues Loubenx de Verdalle was a French knight belonging to the Langue of Provence. He had been La Cassiere's comrade in arms but for some time he had been away from Malta and had few if any pretensions for a grand mastership. But this does not detract an iota from his characteristic love of splendour and domineering attitude which made him enjoy power and glory, as well as the good things of life.

According to the statutes of the Order, in the same way as he could remove a grand master, the Pope was allowed to nominate one, provided this was done after an interregnum of three days. So after the demise of La Cassiere the Pontiff announced to the Convent that they could assemble for an election in the usual way, but before the casting of votes he would reveal his intentions. This announcement was not well received by some of the knights, particularly those of the Spanish Langue who had only one grand master elected from their Langue since the Order's establishment in Malta, and were hoping, indeed endeavouring to have another the more so after the inauspicious end of the rule of the French La Cassiere. They might even have been preoccupied that the Pope would go for another French. Indeed when the knights assembled for the election, the Pope's representative Monsignor Visconti produced a list of three names proposed by the Pontiff. And they were all French. One of them was that of Hugues Loubenx de Verdalle, who was chosen and elected grand master.

Verdalle, as he came to be known, was only 51 and relatively young for the post. He was a typical ecclesiastic, but as already indicated besides being pious he was also worldly. Nonetheless it was not long before it was noted that he was also cunning and a domineering despot, which were qualities only to be surpassed by his love for pomposity and riches. Some of the knights liked him and saw in him the right choice if they were to continue with their resistance to the Inquisitor. Others didn't; particularly the Spanish who continued to be unruly because of their resentment to his nationality.

This did not in the least worry Verdalle who did not hesitate to prohibit the carrying of pistols and daggers in the Auberges considering these to be bandits and assassins' weapons. And henceforth knights could only carry their sword.

But whatever efforts he made in the reorganization of the order, the touch of colour and romance he was destined to give it came after five years of his reign when he was called by Pope Sixtus V who was his personal friend for consultations in Rome. Everyone, including himself thought he was being consulted on the troublesome knights. And there were also those who hinted at some Inquisitor's report. But it was nothing of the sort. Pope Sixtus offered Verdalle to be made a Cardinal and Prince of the Church. It need not be said that being the person he was, Verdalle accepted, and there was certainly a different attitude from that adopted by de Valette when he was also offered the same honour, which he had declined. However pleasantly surprised Verdalle did not know why he was thus singularly selected for this honour, as nobody else did. But there was a school of thought that the Pope might have done it to raise the morale and standing of the Order after its decadence and loss of prestige following La Cassiere's dismal end. There were however speculations that had this been the case, why had the Pope waited for five years? It was soon being realized that it was more likely that as the Pope knew that Verdalle was a close friend of Henry of Navarre who had left the Faith and was then leading the Hugeonots in France, he was hoping that as a Cardinal and Prince his protégée would have a better chance of bringing Henry back to the Faith.

Whatever it was, the Council was aghast at the matter on the return of the grand master to Malta. They had experienced many manipulations from Rome in their time, but never anything like this. More surprised than them was the Inquisitor who would now have to bow to a grand master who was his senior in the hierarchy of the Church. Verdalle was soon in control of the situation, and giving directions as to what was to be done during his absence when he would be going back to Rome for the ceremonial bestowal of his rank. The most troublesome of the knights he silenced by including them in his entourage which was to be made up of eight grand crosses and three hundred knights, all at his own expense.

On his return Malta went en fete. There were flags, gun salvoes and illuminations. But the zenith was reached when the grand master arrived wearing new scarlet robes with the eight pointed cross over his mozzetta. He was the first grand master of Malta to don such robes, as he was to be also the last. The knights met him in their normal black ceremonial mantles, while the Giurati who held his baldachin wore vermilion doublets and plumed hats. The streets of Valletta were packed with people as the grand master arrived at St John's Church for the intonement of a *Te Deum*. Later in the afternoon there was the usual fare of public entertainment. This included the popular *Ġostra* with the competitors having to walk up a greased pole protruding at a slanting angle from a barge to try and reach a flag stuck at the end. All of them would normally slip and drop into the sea to return for another try. The one who manages to reach and pick the flag would be the winner. Another sporting event for healthy men on such occasions was the *Kukkanja* which required competitors to climb with many a difficulty a tall heavily branched pine tree in an attempt to reach the prizes hanging on the top branches.

Verdalle's installation as a Cardinal was no doubt a significant honour for the knights of Malta, and everyone must have been thinking in those days of benefits and advantages the Order would gain. He was not content with just the title and powers of a Cardinal. He wanted to play the role of a Cardinal Prince, as he had seen the role played in Rome. He immediately started with his household where he introduced the elegant fashion of music at dinner, something which would have scandalized the early Hospitallers with their monastic practices. When someone remarked about this to him, Verdalle is quoted as having replied that such music was a foretaste of the sweet strains of Paradise.

His next whim was to build a country retreat where he could escape from the scorching heat of Valletta in summer and snap his fingers at the many problems he had, and would keep having. The motto he aptly adopted for the place was Cedant curae loco – 'let cares surrender to this place. He was no fool and chose one of the best localities in the island where the rocky escarpment he earmarked for his retreat overlooked the only woods and gardens of Boschetto, a paradise of greenery covered with terraces of orange groves and orchards full of trees all the year heavy with loquats and other fruits. And where all throughout the year the place is so redolent of spring with its silent atmosphere broken only by the sweet gurgling waters of natural streams. This earned the place another motto *Ros et pluvia Monte Verdalae* – 'let dew and rain fall on Mount Verdala.' Grand Master Jean de Valette had also chosen that spot for his hunting pastime, and he had built a humble hunting lodge there, but the lordly Verdalle wanted something worthy of a Cardinal prince. So he built Verdala palace. More than a palace this was a fortified country residence, built four square and solid, flanked with four pentagonal towers set at cross angles with the corners to offer fuller resistance to winds. The lovely creamy stone was quarried from the ditch, while the gardens were made up from shiploads of earth and soil brought from Sicily. However martial and feudal the outside of the castle might have looked, the interior contained vast apartments fitted up and decorated to the owner's princely

Verdala Palace, built by Grand Master de Verdalle in the vicinity of Rabat as a country retreat

tastes, such as the frescoes glorifying his spectacular career from youth done by the Florentine painter Paladini, and the monumental bust of himself in the entrance hall.

It cannot be denied that Verdalle had endowed the Order and the country with an outstanding patrimony. So much so that Verdala palace continued to be used by British and Maltese heads of state after the time of the knights, and even in these very days, more than 400 years after it was built, it is still a showpiece used by the President of Malta, and VIPs.

It appears as if Verdalle's choice and idea of his lavish castle gave ideas to Inquisitor Visconti. Under the pretence that inquisitors too suffered from the heat of summer in their palace at Vittoriosa, Visconti built a summer residence in the country-side. He chose a rocky ledge at the head of a fertile valley which ran parallel with Boschetto where Verdalle had built his palace. As if the contrast between the Inquisitor and the Order was indeed a psychological one and not of soul. Nonetheless Verdalle's enemies, mostly the disgruntled Spanish and Italian knights, found enough ground for complaint. Whether it was because of the cost of construction, and this when the people of Malta were poor and suffering, or because he would often seek relief from his gout in a game of cards with some knights. But Verdalle could not care less, and more in a dignified manner than in anger he always had an answer to their complaints. Even when these were referred to the Pope. It was then his turn to react by calling his accusers querulous, morose and vagabonds. One case he didn't win was when he set up a 'favourite nephew' Fra Commander de Segreville and showered on him dignities and emoluments quite in the Apostolic style and for which he was authorized by his friend Pope Sixtus. There were no immediate complaints from his usual enemies, but when he appointed de Segreville as Turpolier of the English Langue, there were objections from another English knight, Wise, and eventually the nephew was shorn of this and other titles.

His greed for riches however, was to gain him even more troubles and worries. It had at that time in the sixteenth century become the habit of countless gentlemen of the highest respectability from foreign countries particularly England to become financially interested in privateering, a business which was only distinguished from piracy with difficulty. The difference between the two being that while a privateer waged war at his own expense and risk against the enemies of his country, with a good part of the captured booty going to the state, a pirate went pillaging on his own to shoulder what gains or losses he made. Privateering in the broadest sense of the term had become an English business as well as a sport, and hundreds of ships were dabbling in it at the time. Profits were good and strict conventions governed how these were to be distributed. Verdalle might have found inspiration in these gentlemen-adventurers amongst them the English Sir John Hawkins, and Sir Francis Drake who had just been knighted by Queen Elizabeth in the way of approval of such exploits. But if there was indeed such inspiration, Verdalle's scope was different. The English gentlemen's motives had been a mixture of adventure in the spirit of Renaissance, patnotism explained in a desire to cripple England's enemies, trade with Spanish possessions from which Philip II tried to exclude all but his own subjects, and reprisals for the ill-treatment of English seamen caught by Spaniards and handed over to the Inquisition to be tortured and burnt. All these always coupled with the capture of booty, with the state and the Queen (in secret) sharing in the spoils. The grand master meant to have his own private galleys to raid and pillage on the high seas with all the booty going into his private coffers.

His friends discouraged him from doing it and brought to his attention the fact that de Valette had tried to obtain permission to do this which was refused because it was contrary to the Order's laws. It is to be said too that the Order at the time was not at war with anyone and rather than being seen as privateering Verdalle's intentions could be more qualified to be considered as piracy. But notwithstanding all this he was adamant and continued to be thrilled and attracted by the gold, silver and precious stones he could lay his hands on. Without asking for anyone's permission he became so bold that he fitted out five ships, and without further ado sent them out on his first venture. But this failed. His first vessel under a Spanish cavalier was seized at Candia with all its booty and crew. Another under Chevalier Bardane was captured by the Turks, while two smaller vessels were shipwrecked off the Barbary Coast. The fifth one did not bring him a fraction of what he was expecting. Any normal person would have given up. But not Verdalle. Totally undismayed he equipped a galiot, and this time sent it forth with four other galleys of the Order with instructions that he would take half the booty they would bring for himself.

Even this venture met with misfortune when the ships encountered two Turkish galleys. A fight ensued during which the captain of Verdalle's galiot kept back and this gave the opportunity to the Turks to escape. To make matters worse, while returning to Malta, the vessels were pounced upon by Venetian galleys, and two of the Order's ships were captured. Only the two remaining galleys returned to Malta, and to Verdalle's dismay carrying less than half the booty that had been captured. This time the grand master was furious. A scapegoat had to be found, and Verdalle had Avogadro the captain of his galley imprisoned. Then to give vent to his temper he began to build two new galleys of his own to resume his privateering as he called it, but which in fact was piracy.

Verdalle did not care that he was now rousing the disapproval of the gentry, and the frowns of statesmen. More than this there was also to be considered the disapproval of the Maltese people by now going through a very lean period of poverty and illness. An epidemic was sweeping the island. Some historians called it the plague, but it was not plague at all. It was more an illness like influenza which nonetheless killed about three thousand and left many others destitute. The Prince now began to be hated by the many paupers he had created. And the Inquisition found a scope to be on watch against the corroding rebellions of the mind. As had happened before there were reports made about him to the Pope. Whether these originated from knights or the Inquisition is not known. But Verdalle always found the right answers to give to his friend Pope Sixtus. His general comment to the Pontiff was: 'Pay no attention to the accusations of my enemies.' And all seem to have gone unheeded. It is no wonder then that when his two new ships were ready, Verdalle lost no time in fitting them for further privateering. When there appeared to be some difficulty in finding the right crew, he helped himself to sailors from the Order's navy, and finished by sending his ships to plunder, while those of the Order remained tied up and idle in port. It was only after Pope Sixtus died that more complaints were raised with the Holy See, and this time the new Pope, Clement VIII had to investigate.

It would not be correct to leave the impression that the Cardinal Prince Verdalle who could bamboozle friend and foe alike where his worldly nature and lust for money were concerned stopped there. It has already been mentioned that besides being worldly he was also a pious man, and his many escapades were very often interspaced with charitable deeds. He was in fact the grand master to encourage the foundation of the Capuchin Order in Malta, as he also promoted Bishop Gargallo's Jesuit College which a later grand master was eventually to turn into the University of Malta. Even such an important establishment had a difficult start for the simple reason that the Bishop wanted the college to be at Notabile (Mdina) while the knights insisted it should be at Valletta. And that was where it was established. With the knights having it their way, one did not expect any further trouble. But eventually the Jesuits fell into disfavour in the Convent because their confessors became too influential in the palace to suit the knights. Verdalle was also instrumental in continuing the work started by his predecessor on a house of solitude for women. But then he also established the Ursuline Convent in Valletta under the protection of the Hospitallers.

There had always been the belief that there was a place for women in the tradition of Orders of Chivalry. The Convent of the Blessed Gerard in fact had maintained a hospital for women as well as for men, and also an affiliated Order of nuns wearing the eight-pointed cross who took vows of Obedience to the Master of the Hospital. It was now that Verdalle took this matter up and after establishing the Ursuline Convent mentioned above, obtained a papal decree which placed those Ursuline nuns under the absolute jurisdiction of the grand master and gave them the Rule of St Benedict which was the same one as the knights. Verdalle built them a convent in Valletta (which still exists today) and endowed them with an estate and rich revenues. As it was also laid down that they were to be provided with free corn, oil and wine by the Religion, and be also allotted a portion of the booty captured by the Order's galleys.

These might have all been considered as beneficial endowments for the Order and posterity, but they did not enhance its popularity beyond the Maltese shores. What became popular in European countries was the grand master's vanity with his specially made scarlet robes as a prince and cardinal in contrast with his predecessors in their austere black robes relieved only by the white eight-pointed cross on breast and left shoulder. And the ducal circlet he added to his coat of arms. There was also curiosity about the extent of his fortune, but none of this affected the Order positively. So much so that notwithstanding its hard rule of celibacy it had always been considered that admission to the Order was a privilege to which European noblemen could aspire, it seems that at the time of Verdalle it could also be considered as a penalty. This was suggested by a dispatch which appeared in The Fugger Newsletter of 9 February 1590 which concerned the discredited alchemist Mamugnano who was granted absolution by the Pope on the conditions that he would make a donation of five thousand crowns, and enter the Order of the knights of Malta.

The end of Verdalle's days came well before it had been expected. He had completely lost the grip of his knights. And these impeached him and had him arraigned before the Holy Office for luxurious living, misappropriation of the Order's funds, and conduct verging on heresy. The charges were dismissed. But the wound caused by his knights was too deep for healing and left him broken hearted. Nonetheless he never shed his obsession for riches. He had never denied he had acquired a large fortune throughout his grand mastership, but then he argued till the end that when enriching himself he was also enriching the Order. And indeed he defied his opponent's right to the last moments on his death-bed because notwithstanding his rights to dispose of his Quint, by which he could dispose of one-fifth of his property by will outside the Order, he refused to do this. When he died in 1595, he left all his vast fortune to the Order.

Grand Master Hugues Loubenx de Verdalle (1582–95)

12

INTO THE SEVENTEENTH CENTURY

The Order of St John had during the first six decades of its stay in Malta very often existed on the tolerance and affection of other states because of its military strength and the island's strategic position. In turn, such states had during the reign of Grand Master Verdalle become too occupied with their own troubles to bother about others. Philip II of Spain who had in his time become the most powerful monarch in the world had sacrificed all for his self-appointed task of starting a counter Reformation intended to destroy Protestantism with his ideals fizzling out after the defeat suffered by his armada in 1588. France had to go through the troubles of three brother kings who all died childless between 1559 and 1589. With the throne being eventually taken by Henry IV better known as Henry of Navarre, the old friend of Verdalle who on the instigation of Pope Sixtus V had in his time unsuccessfully tried to bring him back to the Catholic faith. Pope Sixtus himself, then so close to Verdalle had died in 1590 and brought to an end a more than normal attachment to the Order. England too was busy asserting the prowess of its naval power started by Sir Francis Drake who defeated the Spanish Armada in 1588, and died in 1596. With none of these states being at war with Islam, military interests were soon switching from the Mediterranean to the English Channel and the Atlantic and this pushed the Order out of the limelight making it incumbent on the knights to resume their traditional role of raids against the Barbary pirates and Turkish corsairs which Verdalle had taken away from them and made his own. There had to be this kind of revival if the Order was to regain its name and status.

It was against this background that Grand Master Martin Garzes succeeded Verdalle in 1595. Being a Spaniard it was believed that his election would provide the expected impetus to the Spanish knights and bring to an end their garrulous behaviour. But it seems that these were now ready to resign themselves with their brethren from the other Langues to a more convenient sort of life. By putting aside all national piques ignoring what differences and quarrels there might have been between their countries, and try to dwell in Malta in perfect amity between them.

The Aragonese Grand Master Martin Garzes, 1595 – 1601

They followed the news from all parts of the world, but they left it to their fellow countrymen at home to sustain their quarrels. Much as this helped to keep order amongst them, it was not enough to bring the wanted revival. This needed a strong man to force it. And Martin Garzes was not that kind of man.

It was in his time however that the Order found it necessary to institute its first Board of Admiralty which consisted of an admiral, the captain general of the galleys, and four knights grand cross. Instituted in 1596 it possessed a full secretarial presided over by a general secretary who submitted decisions, proposals and the Accounts of the Navy before the Council of the Order. This Board could now control Christian corsairs who operated upon a written warrant from the viceroy of Sicily, often not being particular about the nationality and flag of their victims. The Order's archives mention two of such reckless buccaneers – Colo Fardello and Canga Rossa, who was eventually hanged by the knights for attacking a Christian merchantman.

It could be that the grand master was more inclined to tie his wagon to the first flashes of the revival of the Renaissance that in his time began to appear in Europe. Indeed Italy had started this movement in the sixteenth century after the Church had lost the grip it had on human interests since the Middle Ages, and men begun more worldly. Not in the way Verdalle had been, but in a bigger rush for knowledge and all that was beautiful in life. Now in England the arts had begun to flourish with the versatility of men like Spenser, Sir Walter Raleigh and William Shakespeare, characterizing the shape of things to come. It could have been because of this tendency that Martin Garzes turned his eyes to embellishing St John's Church by providing the handsome choir-stalls for the Church in 1598. But whatever reason there might have been behind it, fate seems to have looked kindly on the Order when Garzes died three years later at the beginning of the seventeenth century and made way for a better grand master.

The French Alof de Wignacourt who succeeded him in 1601 was also an accomplished lover of art, but this took second priority to his determination to save the Order from the road of transition it seemed to have taken. On being elected grand master he inherited many problems, the most serious being the shortage of water in Valletta which by now was housing a good section of the Maltese population, and an approaching shortage of grain which was the main stay of food for the people of Malta. As water was abundant in the higher areas of the north-west round Mdina the old capital, Wignacourt decided immediately on a system that would conduct some of this water to where it was more needed in the city of Valletta. It was not easy to get water to Valletta. The first engineer that was brought by the Order managed only to get the water, through underground channels to Attard. He left afterwards as he could not solve the technical problems that he met there. Another engineer, Bontadino dei Botnadini, was brought to Malta and through his efforts the water was finally brought into Valletta. Amongst many other fountains, there was one that was set up in Palace Square, as a memento of that important achievement and event. The Order had to fork out a sum equivalent to £3,000 for this project, which was not enough. The rest was paid by Wignacourt from his private funds. But even while dealing with this matter, the grand master also gave his attention to the other more serious question of grain. He couldn't buy any as the state was short of money. What money

Grand Master Alof de Wignacourt (1601–22)

could be spared was being devoted to the building and re-equipment of the Order's navy which had deteriorated during Verdalle's reign. Wignacourt managed to fit up ten galleys with 200 knights and 800 Maltese soldiers, and on 7 April 1603 this force was sent to attack Patras and Lepanto in Greece. The knights captured the two towns on the 20th without encountering any resistance, but found very little if any grain. Fortunately enough however, on their way back to Malta they encountered two Turkish galleys which they captured and these were found to be carrying the wanted grain, besides a good supply of ammunition. And they were brought to Malta to the rejoicing of the people.

There had been few if any occasions when the Maltese people had reason to rejoice openly and genuinely with the knights about some exploit as they did on that day. These were now men and women of two new generations who had learned of the first knights and how by degrees these had obliterated in all but name the ancient privileges of Malta only through what information was handed down from their forefathers. They had come to know as well how knightly vows of poverty and in some cases also of chastity had throughout the years receded into the background, and how the Order seemed to have gradually become more diplomatic than militant. But notwithstanding any ill feelings against the knights they might have been imbued with, they had generated fresh hopes of revival in Wignacourt, and the exploit by the galleys of the Order had realized such hopes in that it signified the Order's interest in their well being, and its return as a maritime power. In 1607 then the dignity of grand master was conjoined with the title of Prince of the Holy Roman empire, by the Pope.

Truly enough Wignacourt continued to send his navy on raids to the Barbary Coast, and what booty was brought back helped to some extent raise the standard of living of the people. But he was also trying to control the many whims of the knights which had continued from the times of previous grand masters. It was therefore in 1604 that to alleviate their idleness he proposed to the chapter-general which accepted to allot chapels to the individual Langues at St John's Church to be made up and decorated accordingly. This had the desired effect and the knights of the various Langues began to compete with one another in an effort to make their particular chapel the most ornate and beautiful. The result of this competition can still be seen and admired to these very days.

In another effort to help the population Wignacourt continued to support the Monte di Pietà, which was set up by the previous grand master, and which was the official pawn broking institution which was the official pawn broking department. It was then also most fitting to include in the same building another institution known as the *Monte della Redenzione degli Schiavi*. This was set up after a Father Raphael, a monk of the Capuchin Order established at the time of Verdalle, was preaching at St John's Church in 1607 and called upon his hearers to inaugurate a fund for the redemption of Christian captives of the Barbary States. Wignacourt reacted positively, and with the money that was soon coming in he set up this Monte di Redenzione. A sum of 70 scudi began to be paid for the return of a Maltese slave, while it had to be 150 scudi for a knight. Subsequently these rates were raised to 200 and 500 scudi respectively, while the two properties were combined.

By time this institution acquired much property all over the island all being adorned with a shield representing three crowns surmounted by the letter 'R' for Redenzione, with the most important of such properties being Selmun palace, also still standing to these very days, and used as a hotel.

It was at about this time that a knight suggested to Wignacourt that he should bring over to Malta one of the greatest and most innovative painters of the Seicento, Michelangelo Merisi who was better known from his birthplace in Italy as Caravaggio. It is not clear who was the knight, but it must have been either Fra Stefano Maria Lomellini who was then paying for the decoration of the new oratory at St John's, or Fra Ippolito Malaspina who was to commission the paintings for the chapel of the Langue of Italy. Some even suggest it could have been some member of the family which went by the name of Gustiniani who had already been patrons of Caravaggio, and who were then preparing an embassy to Grand Master Wignacourt. Whoever it was however who introduced him, Caravaggio was accepted by Wignacourt who had the 38-year-old artist brought over from Italy at about the beginning of 1608 after he had obtained a special Papal authority to receive the painter into the Order.

On his arrival in Malta, Caravaggio painted two portraits of Wignacourt, one in his outstanding armour and another in his magisterial robes. Caravaggio was then received into the Order as a Knight of Obedience and asked to paint his greatest masterpiece *The Beheading of St John*, and a smaller picture of *St Jerome*. One of the aims of the temperamental artist was to become a member of the prestigious Order of St John. For that he had to stay more than a year in Malta, in order for him to be admitted. During his stay on the island, he also continued to paint and befriend other Italian knights. Unfortunately, soon after he was admitted as a member of the Order, he was involved in a fight with a high ranking knight, and this led to his arrest in Fort St Angelo. Yet, he managed somehow to escape from this prison and make his way to Sicily.

No amount of investigations that were carried out, and the Criminal Commission that was set up, composed of knights Jean Honoret and Blasio Suarez under the Maestro Scudiero, could throw a light on how Caravaggio had escaped. But it had become more than obvious that his escape had been engineered by the knights who

Michelangelo Merisi da Caravaggio, Knight of Malta (1571–1610)

had shown that after all they were also masters in what was then called the technique of 'Arrangamento'.

The trial of the painter 'in absentia' was held between 6 October and 1 December 1608. The ceremony of the unfrocking of a knight took place in the oratory of the Beheading of St John, in the same place where the newly inaugurated canvas by Caravaggio was supervising the same proceedings. Caravaggio soon lost his status as a knight, and this must have been another setback in his search for recognition within the higher echelons of society.

A more preoccupied man was Wignacourt who it turned out after the trial had squandered his Divine and Papal Authorization on a common criminal. Something which he had indeed realized in the first place and which, as many believe, made him make all the arrangements for Caravaggio's escape to prevent a hue and cry.

Contrary to expectations there was further news of the Italian painter, roaming from one town to another in Sicily and Naples, until he died a natural death at Porte Ercole two years later.

Wignacourt was considered to have been one of the few grand masters to go down in history as having brought prosperity to the Maltese people, and raised

The Beheading of St John *by Caravaggio*

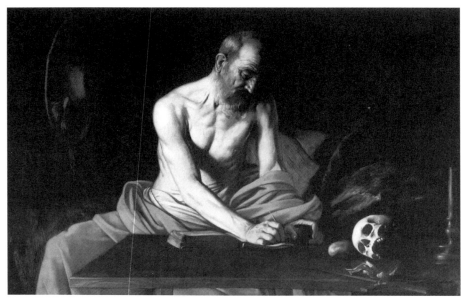

St Jerome *(1607) by Caravaggio*

their standards. He also cared for the Order's heritage where books, manuscripts and similar documents were concerned. According to its statute, the property of deceased knights accrued to the Order. But books and manuscripts were liable to be sold in the absence of a communal library to contain them. This was a pity since many of the knights, indeed almost all of them, possessed such valuable material which stood to be dispersed after their demise. Wignacourt remedied this state of affairs by passing a statute in 1612 prohibiting its dispersal until a library was to be established to take it.

He was also the one to reassert the Order's maritime and military prowess which earned again the esteem of Europe. Even though he might have had a second scope of keeping his knights active and away from sloth and sin, the grand master did not relax a moment with his raids on the Barbary Coast during 1610. But his climax came when in the following year the Order's fleet was sent to attack and plunder the city of Corinth. This hurt the Turks so much that there were soon plans being made to vindicate this attack on a grand scale.

Like de Valette, Wignacourt also had his spies, and it was not long before he learned of the Turks' intentions. Not being the man to make things in half measures he began thinking in terms of another siege, so he put everything aside and began to concentrate on defensive measures. This explains why there were no more new social and cultural benefits for the Order and the country after 1611 during his reign. He was proved to be correct in his assumptions, for the Turks kept their word and appointment. A force of sixty galleys full of troops appeared off Marsaxlokk in the south of Malta on 6 July 1614. The alarm was given and according to the plans laid down, all the population was sent to take cover inside fortified areas which were now more available than in 1565. Then Wignacourt sent out forces of his cavalry to intercept the Turks at Marsaxlokk. But either in the way of strategy or because they did not want to cross swords with the knights that appeared on the spot, the Turks did not land. Instead they moved their galleys to Marsascala and before the knights realized what was happening, they landed a force of 5,000 men there. By the time the Order's forces arrived, the Turks had marched and spread out towards Marsaxlokk and Zejtun robbing and setting fire to farms and houses they found in their way. When the knights' cavalry made contact, the Turks refused to give battle and withdrew. But in the small skirmishes that took place, the knights captured some sixty prisoners.

The defenders on the fortifications of Valletta and Grand Harbour then saw the Turkish fleet go past. Slowly and steadily as if reconnoitring before deciding to attack. But no attack materialized. The next news came from Mellieħa on the northern tip of Malta where some of the Turks landed, more likely to take water, rather than to fight, and from where they were soon removed by Maltese soldiers.

Some argue that Turkish intentions might have only been in terms of a simple raid on that occasion. On the other hand the size of their force was more consistent with an attack and a long battle. One may therefore safely assume that they had a change of mind on realizing the revived military strength of the Order and improved fortifications of the island. It was a feather in Wignacourt's cap, and under him the knights continued to police the Mediterranean, setting free Christian captives, and seeking out corsairs, collecting slaves and hostages many of whom were ransomed for gold to swell even further the Order's coffers, as if in anticipation of the good times that had to come. These however Wignacourt failed to see, since he died in 1622.

*   *   *

Very little came to be known of his Portuguese successor Luis Mendez de Vasconcellos. His election was characterized by a tiff he had with the Church in his first months of office when he objected to the erection of a palace in Valletta by Bishop Cagliares on the grounds that this would facilitate interference with his jurisdiction by the Ecclesiastical Authorities. But after an appeal to Rome, permission was granted to the Bishop with the condition however that this court or 'Curia Vescovile' as it was called would remain in the old city of Mdina. Soon after, in 1623 Vasconcellos died, leaving for posterity his portrait, devoid of any emblem of sovereignty, but complete with crucifix and book of devotions as if in confirmation of his piety and goodness which would certainly not have made him the right man to rule the Order in the turbulent years that were to follow.

Maybe one can mention that the year 1622 brought to the fore one of the most hard working knights. The German Christian Osterhausen took a very active part in the service of the Convent. This year he was put on a special commission to prepare the official programme and protocol for a visit being made to Malta by the French

101

Duke of Beaufort. The year after, Osterhausen was chosen to settle a dispute that arose amongst the nursing staff of the Sacra Infirmeria, the Order's hospital. This was only a beginning, and the German knight was to be given more important assignments which reflect not only the increasing ardour of the knights but also the various commitments the Order had to undertake.

The successor to Vasconcellos was the French Antoine de Paule. This new grand master was a vain and self-indulgent person more determined for a reign of soft living rather than that of following scrupulously what good examples had been set by his predecessors. Perhaps more than by his beginning he can be better judged by his end after a reign of twelve years. And his judge could not be other than the Inquisitor at the time, Fabio Chigi, who subsequently became Pope Alexander VII. 'The grand master is dying,' he had written during De Paule's last days, 'but without altering irreverence, his sensuality, his duplicity, his selling of favours, his twisting of justice after his own fashion, and his saying that 'briefs and citations were priests' stock-in-trade', as he was also indifferent to censure.'

That was in a nutshell the description of the grand master's character, and a likely question to be justifiably raised is how and why such a person had to be elected as grand master? The answer could be found in an allegation made by his knights during one of their complaints to the Pope on 11 May 1631, that De Paule had bribed and corrupted in order to get himself elected.

His vanity can still be gauged till these days by the palace and gardens he built for himself and named after his patron saint. San Anton palace had even after the knights left Malta become the regular residence of Malta's rulers, and until these days it houses the President of Malta. The gardens have become public. If De Paule was trying to emulate Verdalle then he went one better with the dinner he gave for 600 guests on the day of his installation at the palace. According to records still in Malta, the guest list was not in any way restricted, but besides friends and important personages it included his game-keepers, falconers, drummers and trumpeters, valets, grooms and domestics, as well as the wig-makers, and even the rat-catcher.

Justifiably enough De Paule had gone down in history as the grand master who had started soft living at the headquarters of the Order, but this cannot be taken as having brought it into disrepute in Europe. His shortcomings were only internal affairs, and if he qualified as a tyrant, then he was a benevolent one. He might have found his finances with a small regard for legality but country and people got their share. He also tried 'to maintain the Order's prowess on the high seas, although an expedition he sent against the Turks around 1628 was not as successful as he might have desired. There were five galleys sent out to attack St Maura, one of the Ionian Islands on that occasion, which was in the hands of the Turks. A desperate battle ensued, and the Order's galleys were made to return to Malta with 180 slaves. However on their way back they were attacked by corsairs and after another battle they lost two galleys which were carried away by the enemy to Barbary.

By this time the majority of the people now belonging to a middle class fraternized with the knights and were often their companions in Coffee Shops, receptions and other social occasions. Only the noble and upper classes notwithstanding their association with the knights had remained resentful. As they became aloof from the new middle class since this had emerged from that part of the people in the harbour area on which they had always looked down, even before the arrival of the Order. Yet they had circumvented the refusal to admit their sons into the Order because of their Maltese birth by arranging to have their wives confined in Sicily, and thus a number of Maltese had eventually become members of the Order. Of course there could not be a Maltese Langue, but Maltese knights were accepted into the Italian Langue because of their birth in Sicily, and at least two became grand priors and second only in dignity and influence to the grand master. One of these was Commander Giovanni Francesco Abela who was vice-chancellor of the Order, and also a very discursive writer on Malta of his time.

Irrespective of class and level then, many of the Maltese people took throughout the years to copying the knights' ways of life. They built their houses on the plans of the auberges, and made their clothing as well as organized their domestic habits upon knightly patterns. They even copied their cooking, and some of the common dishes of those times, like *imbuljuta* (chestnuts), sausages and *pastizzi* (cheesecakes) are still considered Maltese delicacies of today. Although some of the old houses had their own bakeries, their cold storage packed with Sicilian snow, their laundries as well as their sewing rooms.

Maybe what inspiration was lacking from Grand Master Antoine de Paule until the end of his reign, was on the other hand coming from his knights. Because notwithstanding their continued indiscipline, behaviour which he could obviously not control, the Order continued to enjoy a good reputation, and was still attracting many young nobles from Europe to join its ranks, presumably all intended to carry out their two year caravan and then enjoy life either in Malta or in the various European commanderies. Some of them who were protégés of important people were destined to do better than others in the Order. One of these was the German Prince Frederick von Hessen. He was the son of Prince Ludwig Landgrave of Hessen who had first visited Malta at the time of Alof de Wignacourt then passed the good impressions he had of the Order on to his son. But much as the young Hessen qualified in the matter of lineage, he could not join the Order as he was not a Catholic. Being the protégé of Cardinal Francesco Barberini who was the nephew of the then reigning Pope Urbanus VIII Hessen was soon coached and instructed in the new religion and became a Catholic. Then he returned to Malta in the following year 1637 to be admitted into the Order. As if this was not enough the Pope bestowed him with the grand cross of Malta. Eventually in time he was also given the title of Cardinal.

What Grand Master Antoine de Paule got from Pope Urban VIII was a black mark of being considered a 'persona non grata' while the knights had to resist the Pope's eventual order to have the Inquisitor preside over the chapter-general of the Order since they contended this to be a limitation of their authority. It was with these internal upheavals that the rule passed to 75-year-old Jean de Lascaris-Castellar, another French, after Antoine de Paule died in 1636.

Coming as it did at a time when the Order needed a strong hand to instil discipline in the young upcoming knights, the election of a 75-year-old grand master might have for some appeared inappropriate. On the other hand one can see the wisdom behind his choice because of his known faithful devotion to the Order and his experience which made him the right person and antidote for its troubles. His determination to undertake the hard tasks ahead can then be further appreciated by the fact that his rule had to begin with a psychological handicap in that it revived a sad episode of another Lascaris who was his kinsman. This fellow was a Phanarrot Greek who had fought with the Turks against the Order in the siege of 1565, but he had eventually changed sides and even betrayed a projected Turkish assault to the knights. Nonetheless he was still considered as a traitor, and his treacherous act was never forgotten with his name continuing to be held in contempt. Some might have even found a fickle connection of this with the grand master's grim features which remained a by-word till present times – as *wiċċ Laskri* depicting a hard and treacherous look.

In truth however, the new grand master was a wise and conscientious person who set his heart on his major task of bringing progress to the Order after the lapses of his predecessor. Immediately following his election he took in hand the completion of fortifications outside Valletta which De Paule had started under the direction of engineer Floriani of Macerata but discontinued because of lack of funds. Indeed, Lascaris had to find ways and means how to borrow money, because the Order's coffers were empty. This was due to the fact that the Thirty Years War (1618–48) had deprived the Order of considerable property and commanderies in Germany. And for twenty years it did not receive a single crown from there. The grand master also planned and completed a wharf in Grand Harbour that joined Valletta to the inner basin of Marsa. This was already a port of some sort. In Arabic, the word means 'port'. Although there is a school of thought it was so called as it was a marsh, where indeed the knights used to hunt duck. But these works were undertaken in the way of improvements which every grand master tried to make in the defensive or administrative structure of the island. Concurrently Lascaris was giving attention to the state of the knights. True to his dedication for which they had indeed elected him he was soon trying to find ways and means on how to curb their inclinations for dice, women and wine. More than that he was a strict disciplinarian. It was during his time that there was some trouble when he forbade women from wearing masks during carnival or to attend dramatic performances in the Auberges. The knights were incensed; not against the grand master but against the Jesuit fathers whom they blamed for this decision, knowing that the grand master's confessor was a Jesuit. Lascaris had to send some of the Jesuits into temporary exile in Sicily to ensure their safety. On the other hand he felt he had to provide an alternative to keep the knights off these vices. So he built them a place where they could play the ball-game called pal Jamaglio. This was located outside Valletta where later there was to be erected the suburb town of Floriana. Then to emphasize his scope he had the enclosed place adorned with a marble tablet with a relevant stanza in Latin which he composed. The translation in English as set down by Sir Harry Luke in his book *Malta – An Account and an Appreciation*, read as follows:-

Here perish sloth, here perish Cupid's arts,
Knights, where on you this strip I now bestow.
Here play your games and steel your warlike hearts,
Not let wine, women, dicing bring you low.

How effective was this move is not known. But Lascaris did not stop there and he was soon building another hospital, this time a Lazzaretto or as it was called a Pest-house to provide the necessary isolation for persons suffering from contagious diseases. Thus killing two birds with one stone for besides supporting the Sacra Infirmeria built by La Cassiere during epidemics which by that time were breaking out more often it also provided the scope and occasions for the knights to carry out their hospitaller duties. In line with the extraordinary dexterity of Lascaris, by now an octogenarian, this hospital turned out to be one of the best organized and with a good reputation around the Mediterranean.

What sense of lassitude and laziness there was in certain elements of the Order cannot of course be attributed to all the knights. There were many of them who throughout all their time were an example of genuine endeavour and fortitude in their convent life. One of them, already mentioned was the German Christian Osterhausen. His qualities were recognized also by Lascaris who gave him several important posts. In 1638 he was appointed Commissioner of the galleys, then in 1639 to 1641 he was Auditor to the Langue of Germany. In 1647 Osterhausen had to review all males between the ages of 16 and 60 in the town of Vittoriosa to be considered for service in the militia. He was assisted in this assignment by the prior of Messina, Flaminio Balbiani, another excellent knight. Other areas were assigned to Franz von Sonnerberg, the pilier of Germany with commander Bottigalla, and Commander Palant with Commander De San Marc. Then with Flaminio Balbiani and the bailiff of Majorca Fra Raphael Cotoner (a future grand master), Osterhausen was commissioned to carry out a health survey of Malta in 1655, after an outbreak of plague at the village of Zejtun.

It may be mentioned that the Order, through Lascaris, did not lose touch with the movement of Renaissance still enveloping Europe and in 1644 there was established the first Printing Press in Malta by Pompeo del Fiore which augured an outburst of literature stimulated as this was, by rediscovered literature of Greece and Rome. It was in this year too that the maritime prowess of the Order, also maintained by Lascaris carried out a remarkable exploit. The Order's galleys while on patrol in the Dodecanese Islands encountered a Turkish convoy escorting a mighty galleon the *Sultana*. They gave battle, and after a terrific fight managed to capture this galleon and brought her to Malta. The value of the captured prize was realized when it was found out that it belonged to the Qizlar Aghasi, chief of the Black Eunuchs who rated as third dignitary of state of the Ottoman empire. But the surprise of the packet was the young woman found amongst the passengers. Her bearing and size of her wardrobe and jewels showed she was a woman of importance. Her name was Zafire and she was accompanied by a two-year-old son. First assumptions were that she was one of the Sultan Ibrahim's favourites and that the boy called Osman was the sultan's own son, but later versions placed her as a slave of Qizlar Aghasi and only a foster mother of the sultan's son who later reigned as Mehmed IV, and who was at the time of the same age as Osman, the captured boy. Whichever was the correct version, the fact remains that Zafire died soon after, and Lascaris took the young boy to be brought up into the Convent where subsequently he was converted to Christianity, and when of age became a monk in the Dominican Order.

Although no historian mentions it, it might have been a decision to avenge the capture of the *Sultana* that made the Turks plan an attack on Malta in the following year. Lascaris came to know about it and became much perturbed. But rather than losing his head he gave the matter all his attention. He knew he had the necessary fortifications to meet an attack, but he didn't have the men. He began to recruit a force of 18,000 men but after the monies he had been spending on his projects, he did not have enough to pay his newly engaged troops and to get the extra armaments and ammunition he needed. So much as it was against his will, he began to collect all the silver he could get to be coined into money. It is believed that no other grand master could have done it, but Lascaris was by now well known by the people for his wisdom and sober ruling, and the necessary silver was found. The people were more aghast and became troublesome when there was a decision that if the Turks attacked, the city of Mdina would be abandoned as it was considered to be untenable. The women of the city immediately crowded the streets, and armed with logs of wood protested against this decision. In the end Lascaris had to submit and promised to withdraw his order.

Fortunately enough the attack never materialized, and the money and silver borrowed began to be repaid back, giving also that little respite the grand master wanted to think about a suggestion proffered by a knight, Chevalier de Poincy, who was Governor of the French part of the island of St Kitts in the West Indies, for the Order to acquire a nucleus of a Colonial empire in that area then considered as the New World. Being still full of enterprise Lascaris was favourably disposed to go ahead. What he temporarily lacked was the money which he was convinced he would find in a few years' time. One small preoccupation he also wanted to settle concerned the quantity of manuscripts and documents left by deceased knights which could not be disposed of according to the statute issued by Grand Master Wignacourt in 1612. Now, 38 years later Lascaris established a library in the vestry of St John's Church to contain all this valuable material.

The only other obstacle which seemed far from being a temporary one was the continued irregular behaviour of his knights, which notwithstanding their respect for him, continued to be unruly. Something, which even with his wisdom and correct ruling he had failed to control. They were always finding their own private ways and means of how to break the law and go against orders. With restrictions still being in force against duelling, they had by now arranged for their own place where they could resort to this activity away from the eyes of law. Strait Street in Valletta, so called because of its narrowness, and hidden between the high buildings of the city suited their purpose. With their seconds guarding both ends of the street to keep out passers-by, duelists could combat freely till first blood was drawn or even till one of them was killed. Even though this venue was only a stone's throw away from the grand masters palace. At that particular time, however, the knights' antagonism was directed against the Inquisitor, 'Monsignor Gio Batta Gannellini Gori who in May 1646 was constrained to beg the Cardinal President of the Holy office in Rome to relieve him of his duties in Malta, as he had been informed that some knights were determined to kill him for having imprisoned their prostitutes. It was not very long after that Lascaris had to write to the Pope, telling him that notwithstanding all that he did, he was finding it impossible to rule over knights of different nations and mentalities.

This was the anticlimax to the rule by one of the best grand masters. But it was not the end. By now a nonagenarian Lascaris decided positively to agree to the suggestion by Chevalier de Poincy, and in 1653 bought off King Louis XIV the Indian Islands of St Croix, St Bartholomew and Tortuga; as well as the French sections of St Kitts and St Martin. His had of course been the wrong decision, because one could hardly see how the knights could bring themselves to run those islands inhabited by coloured people engaged in planting sugar-cane and tobacco, with little if any chance of operating their galleys in that part of the world already notoriously haunted by hundreds of pirates of different nationalities.

But what mattered most to Lascaris then was that the flag of St John would be also installed in the Caribbean, and he must have given little thought on how this would have to be sustained. Certainly not in his time, for he was 92, and much less in the years to follow. The truth is that what little energy remained to him was spent in seeing to the maintenance of his navy, and here at least he was not disappointed in having Chevalier Gregorio Carafa reach the highest level as a sea-captain, and this marked and confirmed by his command of the Order's fleet when he defeated the Turks in 1656 when aiding the Venetians at Candia in what was to become known in history as the Battle of the Dardanelles. Lascaris died in the following year at the age of 96.

The knights were sorry for his loss, and switched all their antagonism on to the Inquisitor whom they knew to be opposing their choice for the next grand master.

St Mary's Tower, Comino, built by Grand Master Wignacourt

Indeed much as he tried to prevent it, the Spanish Martin de Redin was elected grand master to succeed Lascaris. It must have been this sense of pique and antagonism that made the Inquisitor pounce on two English Quaker ladies on 21 December 1658 who had come to Malta at that time of the Restoration to convert the Maltese to their tenets. De Redin could not interfere since the case was considered to be within the jurisdiction of the Inquisitor who also tried in various ways to dissuade the two ladies from carrying on with their mission. But nothing would divert Catherine Evans and Sarah Chevers from carrying out what they considered to be their divine duties. They were confined to a prison which nonetheless did not detract their efforts to preach and try to convert passers-by from the window of their prison where they were kept throughout the grand master's reign.

Much as De Redin could count on his knights' support in encouraging the waves of the Renaissance that were now so compelling, he missed his chances when from the first year of his reign he wanted to put right one particular element of defence. Valletta and the Grand Harbour area where most of the population lived were properly fortified and defended. But the same could not be said for the coast so he devised and built a girdle of thirteen watch towers as characteristic of their epoch as the Martello Towers on the south coast of England. Their purpose was to guard against sudden raids, being located in such a way that guards keeping watch could on seeing the enemy flash their signals from one to the other until these reached the capital.

St Paul's Bay Tower

But De Redin did not live to see the usefulness of his towers, which were a permanent legacy to the Maltese archipelago. He died in 1660, to be succeeded by the French Annet de Clermont-Gessan, a name which proved to be longer than his reign, since he died after three months of his grand master ship. As if both of them to hasten the coming of Renaissance to Malta.

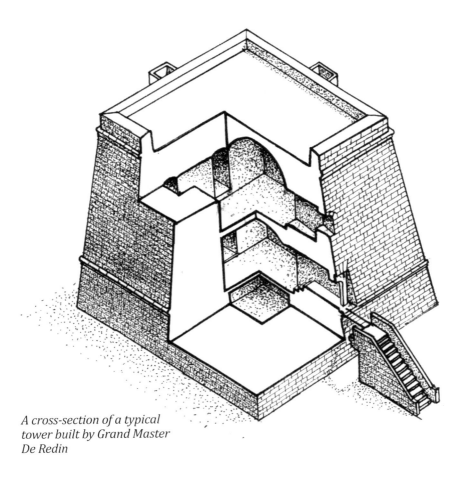

A cross-section of a typical tower built by Grand Master De Redin

13

DECADES OF THE RENAISSANCE

By the turn of the seventeenth century a new artistic movement had been born. This was Baroque, which was to be the central focus of the activities of the Order in Malta in all spheres of life. During the Baroque period, the knights decorated their churches and palaces, rebuilt their own residences and places of worship with new buildings, as well as used baroque mentality even in the defence of the islands. This shows that the Order was keeping abreast of what was happening in Europe. At the beginning of the seventeenth century, architecture started to move away from the austere style that was still predominant in Malta, after the arrival in Malta of the Italian architect Francesco Buonamici. Later on in the century, there arrived in Malta Mattia Preti, an Italian artist who was to dominate the artistic scene for the rest of the century. In 1661 there was chosen as the new grand master, Raphael Cotoner, who was to start in earnest the decoration of the interior of the Conventual Church of the Order, and which was continued throughout the reign of his brother, Nicholas, who succeeded him in 1663.

Fortunately enough there was no trouble coming from the Turks at the time, and with the exception of a small addition to that part of Valletta's fortifications overlooking Grand Harbour, Raphael Cotoner spent all the money he could afford on artistic works. His first attention in this regard was to the Sacra Infirmeria, the hospital of the Order, by now well renowned throughout Europe, and which might have become too small for its wide patronage. The grand master had it remodelled and enlarged. Separate wards were built for surgical and medical cases. Fever and dysentery patients were isolated while there was accommodation provided for convalescents. Special wards were provided for mental cases. The insane were until then put in prison. There was also introduced the luxury of single beds, and this when having two or three patients in the same bed was still customary in Europe. He also established a school of Anatomy and Surgery at the hospital with a library. Then he began to concentrate his efforts on embellishing St John's Conventual Church. Much as the various Langues had made and adorned their chapels there was still a

The magnificent interior of St John co-cathedral

lot to be done to make the church the Valhalla it was intended to be. And there could not have been a better time to do it than now, with a grand master being a lover of art, and the knights imbued with the spirit of Baroque. So Raphael Cotoner engaged the Calabrian artist Mattia Preti to start the decoration of the vault of the Conventual Church, besides becoming the overall artistic director of the Order in Malta. Preti was also commissioned to do many other canvases in the same church, and he also executed other paintings for other churches around the islands.

Preti was not another Caravaggio. Truly enough he was like him accepted into the Order, and was also rewarded during the various stages of his work. But he made an excellent job of his frescoes which gave St John's Church an exceptional splendour which can still be admired till these very days. Preti had also offered to do the great vault at his own expense, and this is authenticated by the Archives of the Order (A.O.M. 260 f.106 of 15 September 1661) when he made the offer, and further

St Helen's Gate, Cospicua

confirmed in the same archives (A.O.M. 260 f.108 of a fortnight later) when his offer was accepted. On 9 August 1663 then, Preti was commissioned to gild the pillars of the chapel of the Langue of Castile in the same church, this time at the expense of the Order. This was the last work to be undertaken by the painter for Raphael Cotoner who died in that same year.

His brother Nicolas who succeeded him continued where he had left, and Mattia Preti was further commissioned to paint and gild various other parts of St John's Church. Not only this, but after finishing the benefactions of this church he was soon painting altar-pieces for other churches, the most extensive one of which being done for the old conventual church of St Lawrence in Vittoriosa depicting the martyrdom of the saint, still resplendent today, even though mellowed by time. Preti also painted various pictures for secular palaces, thus carrying even further the spirit of Renaissance into Malta and to her people. He was to continue in his useful work until he died at the age of 86 in 1699 and was fittingly buried in St John's Church which he had so stupendously adorned.

One cannot help noticing that during this time very little if any lamenting emerges about the dubious conduct of the knights. This may reflect the grand master's popularity who had been elected by them unanimously. At the same time there is ample evidence in the Order's archives of the many donations made by knights to St John's Church. There were organs, silver candlesticks, a niche and two silver statues. It seems as if the knights of Malta might have then found more scope for their vows by getting involved in the spirit of the Renaissance. The one point which stood to their credit was the realization of the futility of the dream of an empire started by Lascaris. In the same way as this grand master had acquired islands in the West Indies in 1653, now in 1665 grand master Nicolas Cotoner divested the Order of this property even if he had to lose money on such useless encumbrances. All the property was sold to the West Indies Company for 500,000 livres Tournois which was not even half their original value.

That same year the grand master prevailed upon his Council to ask the Maltese sculptor Melchior Gafà who was then in Rome to pay a visit to Malta with a view of embellishing the Niche of St John in the Conventual Church. This in fact materialized on 23 January 1666 when the sculptor's designs were examined by Mattia Preti and Chevalier Blondel and the best of them was accepted on 7 April of that same year. Gafà received a golden chain for his efforts. As it happened a year later the sculptor died.

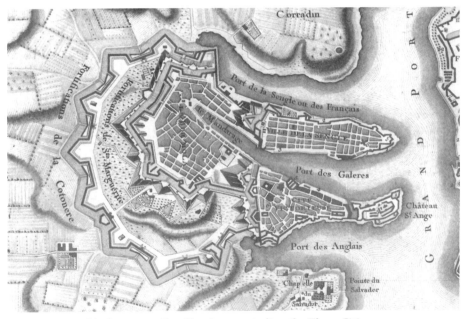

The impregnable Cottonera Fortifications encircling the Three Cities

Nicolas Cotoner's wisdom however may be seen in a better light from his fresh worries about defence. In 1669, Candia fell to the Turks and this made him turn his attention to build further fortifications to enclose in the Grand Harbour's fold the cities of Vittoriosa and Senglea as well as that of Cospicua which had risen between them. But more than a simple line of ramparts, he began building an eloquent system of bastions and demi-bastions, with cavaliers and counterguards, ravelins, lunettes and gates that were eventually to be considered as the most impressive monuments in Europe of western military architecture of their time, and a product of the Renaissance. The three enclosed cities within these fortifications then went down into the annals of history by the name of Cottonera after the grand master's name. Where expenses were concerned these fortifications proved to be a bottomless pit. The Treasury could not find all the money required and resort had to be made to the various commanderies. What they contributed too could not pay for everything, and it might have been a blessing in disguise when the engineers met with some difficulties and work had to stop.

There is no doubt that the knights had by this time brought much prosperity to Malta, and raised the standard of living of her people to much above the general European level.

They had also imbued all sections of the population with the ethical sense of behaviour appertaining to their particular standing in life. Much of this is reflected in the contents of a diary kept by the Reverend Henry Teonge, Vicar of Spernall in Warwickshire, England, who visited Malta in August, 1675 when he was chaplain on *HMS Assistance* which formed part of the naval squadron which British Admiral Sir John Narborough took to the island at that time. This official visit materialized after Britain became perturbed by the troublesome Turks who after capturing Crete from the Venetians began again to harass shipping of Christian powers in the Mediterranean. In 1674, King Charles II of England decided to take action and dispatched the mentioned naval squadron on an expedition against Tripoli, with a break in the journey at Malta. A letter from the King which is still preserved in the National Malta Library commends the admiral and his squadron to the goodwill of the most Eminent Prince and Lord Nicolas Cotoner, grand master of the Order of Malta, our Cousin and dear Friend,' asking him to treat the admiral and his ships in the Order's territory as allies and friends, allowing them to buy their requirements there at a fair price.

Teonge's diary was written in the English of his days, so in reproducing the following extracts I took the liberty of rearranging spelling and construction in the English of today. Otherwise the script is reproduced as it appeared in his diary and eventually used by Sir Harry Luke in his book *Malta – An appreciation*.

1 August 1675 – This morning we came near Malta; or as it was formerly called Melita from the abundance of honey they have there, gathered by the bees from the annice seeds and flowers thereof, which grow on the island abundantly. Before we came to the city, a boat with the Maltese flag came to us to get to know whence we came from. We told them from England, and they asked if we had a bill of health. Our captain told them he had no bill but what was in his guns' mouths. We came on and anchored in the harbour between the old town and the new about 9 o'clock; but we had to wait for the government's leisure before we could go ashore. This was delayed because our captain would not salute the city unless he knew they would respond.

At last the Consul came with his attendants to our ship, but would not come aboard till our captain had been ashore. He told us we could go ashore 6, 8 or 10 at a time and that we could have anything there was to be had, also with a promise to answer our salute. Whereupon our captain took a glass of sack and drank to the health of King Charles. Then he fired a salute of seven guns, which was replied to by another of five guns from the city, and which was more than they had done to all other men-of-war that had come there before. This being done the captain sent his lieutenant to salute the grand master and to tell him that he would wait on him the next morning.

2 August – Accompanied by two more gentlemen I went ashore. I went round the city and viewed the fortifications which I cannot describe with the whole city being as it was on perfect rock, furnished with all brass cannons and not one of iron, some of them 23 feet long. I thought there was no need of any sentries since there was no way of going over the outermost wall. But beyond that there were two wide and deep trenches or dry moats, cut out of the main rock, one within the other and deep enough that they couldn't be filled up, and so wide that none could pass over.

There was an array of men in the centre of the city while for each house there was a castle. The storehouses of corn and other provisions were in the form of wells cut into the main rock 20 fathoms deep and more, and very spacious in the bottom, but narrow at the top and covered with a massive stone closed up with tarras. And then they have them in good numbers and in several places in the city where they have constant corn and all other provisions for three hundred thousand men for 3 years.

The hospital is a vast structure. It is so broad that 12 men may walk abreast with ease between the rows of beds on each side. The beds stand on four iron pillars and white curtains all extremely neat and sweet. It houses 300 beds besides the spacious rooms for the knights and a stately home for the chief doctor and his attendants.

The city is almost surrounded by sea which provides safe harbours for hundreds of ships. The people are generally courteous, but especially to the English.... Several of the knights came on board, 6 at a time, men of sufficient courage and friendly carriage, to wish us a good voyage.

3 August – Here we have excellent wine for 3d. a quart, muskmelons ld. a piece, cotton stocking for 9d. a pair. Notwithstanding the strength of this place, they are daily adding new works especially on the outside of the harbour where they have built big fortifications towards the sea of big strength.

There could not have been a more clear confirmation of what has already been written about the evolvement of Malta and her knights than the simple description of Teonge. Narborough's visit shows that there was already British interest in Malta at the time, while the captain's disrespectful reply regarding the bill of health was indicative of English arrogance. Indeed English knights were always disposed to be so arrogant particularly after the Reformation when their manners excited repugnance to the nobility. Nonetheless the Order held no resentment, and even when it lost property in England there was forgiveness as traditionally preached by religion. It was however a different question in the matter of naval salutes. An incident had already occurred in 1628 when a discourteous English ship towing a Maltese tartana laden with wine failed to haul down her flag in response to a given salute. Much as there was often the remark that the English were tougher than the Turks, the Order held firm on matters of saluting, and after further correspondence it was the English monarch Charles II who had to compromise.

The last fortification which Teonge described as was being built outside the harbour towards the sea was Fort Ricasoli. Nicolas Cotoner decided to build this fort on the entrance of Grand Harbour right opposite Fort St Elmo. As the Order could not afford the expense involved, the money was found partly by the Church and the Knight Bailiff Francesco Ricasoli who forked out the larger part of his property for its construction. The least the Order could do in recompense was to name the fort after him.

Teonge was again in Malta with the return of the British squadron from Tripoli on 12 January 1676. This time however they found a more subdued Malta because of a plague epidemic that was rife and had killed about 12,000 throughout its course. But nonetheless, although they were not allowed to go ashore, Teonge noted many things which merit mentioning. On the launching of a new brigantine he had this to say:

Today (22 February 1676) we saw a great deal of solemnity at the launching of a new brigantine of 23 oars, built on shore and very near the water. They hoisted three flags in her yesterday and today by noon they had turned her head towards the water when a great multitude of people gathered together with several knights and important people, with a crowd of friars and churchmen. There were at least two hours of benedictions in the nature of hymns or anthems with trumpets and other musical instruments being played too often.

Finally two friars and an attendant went into her, and kneeling down prayed for half an hour, laying their hands on every mast and other places of the vessel, and sprinkling her all over with holy water. They then hoisted a pennant to signify she was a man-of-war, and the ship was thrust into the water to a salute of 21 guns before going into the cove where all their galleys lay.

Teonge also mentions some of the measures taken to fight the plague. He says that ships that carried the infection heavily were burnt while a man who was caught stealing goods from houses of those who died of the plague, was hanged. But plague or not, his ship took provisions from Malta, and Teonge's last dinner before departure goes on to confirm the island's standard of living in those days. Teonge says he dined with his friends, probably officers of the ship, and they had a gallant baked pudding, an excellent leg of pork and cauliflowers, an excellent dish made of pigs' pettitoes, two roasted pigs, one turkey cock, a roasted hog's head, 3 ducks, a dish of Cyprus birds, and dessert made of pistachios and dates, washed down by some very good wine.

And this was not an exception. For on the question of food and the style of living in Malta in the seventeenth century there is more evidence forthcoming from a French writer calling himself *un gentil homme* Francois who in 1679 gave a rare brief description of the situation in his work *Nouvelle relation du voyage et description exacte de l'Île de Malte*. He wrote as follows:

I never failed to admire the quantity of the viands that are served and to wonder how so dry and barren a rock can produce such refreshment and so much game.

Every day the market is full of vegetables and of almost every kind of fruit;

the bread is excellent, beef and mutton of a marvellous taste. Veal and poultry are eaten at all seasons, notwithstanding the fact that there is little pasture.

Partridges, pigeons, rabbits, thrushes and other game are fatter than anywhere else in Europe; and although the island lies on the 34th degree, there is no lack of iced dishes and of snow, thanks to the efforts of a contractor who charges two sols six deniers a pound on the understanding that he supplies it all the year round. He brings it from the mountains of Sicily, and pays a fine of nine ecus for every day that he fails to deliver it.

It seems that by this time even the lot of slaves had improved and was certainly not that hard. They were of course still having their head shaved, as they were also expected to be fettered or dragging chains on their feet. But many of them were now being adapted to domestic labour rather than to galleys which began to change from oars to sail. Even so, the slave population had become so big that something had to be done to utilize them. Some of them were now earning money by working in the Hospital, the Bakery or the Treasury. Others were taken as porters to carry sedan chairs used by old bailiffs. There were many of them who could weave cloth for sails, or make wicker baskets. Others could peddle hot pastry or bake bread, also repairing shoes or carved wood. Some of them were also making a good living by shaving the Jesuits.

Some historians attribute the beginning of soft living by the knights of Malta to Grand Master Antoine de Paule (1623–36). This could have been true, but life in the Order could by the latter part of Nicolas Cotoner's reign be better described as being one in which the grand master had developed into one of the Western ruling Princes. That he was in fact considered as one can be deduced by the amount of correspondence with the crowned heads of Christendom throughout time. Right from the first Holy Roman Emperors, the Tudors, Stuarts and early Georges of England, right through rulers of France and the Iberian Peninsula to Princes of the German and Italian states and Doges of Venice. We have seen the letter of the English Charles II to Nicolas Cotoner on the question of the British expedition to Tripoli. All this forms a unique picture of the transmutation of the Order into something well outside its original scope. Therefore Inquisitor Marescoti must have been right when he wrote to Pope Alexander VIII saying that the Order had lost its former fervour and had become exceedingly worldly.

The Pope reacted and was soon pressing on Cotoner to cut down on worldly living and revert to what was more in the Order's traditional commitment. The Pontiff was troubled by the recapture of Candia by the Turks in 1669, and had since then been trying to mount a relief expedition without success. Now, in 1680 he was proposing to Cotoner to give up thinking about the celebration of Carnival and give his attention to ways and means of how to relieve Candia.

But there was little if any chance for Cotoner to oblige. Apart from the fact that the Order's navy had not indulged in any big naval battle since that of the Dardanelles in 1656 during the time of Lascaris, he was now an ailing man at the age of 75. Much as he continued to rule as a royal monarch brooking no opposition, and reducing passions and jealousies of opponents to obsequiousness, he knew that his days were numbered. He now had to be carried in a sedan chair to all his functions. But he still carried on with the celebration of Carnival that year. However during Holy Week

Mdina metropolitan cathedral

which falls six weeks later although feeling sick and listless he also participated in the traditional functions of washing the feet of the twelve men dressed as the Apostles on Maundy Thursday, and carried out the Visits to the Seven Churches. But that was all he could do. A week later he was dead.

✳   ✳   ✳

One wonders whether there might have been papal influence in the election of the Italian Gregorio Carafa to succeed Nicolas Cotoner. Carafa was an upright man and had many good qualities to qualify him as grand master which of course some other knights might also have had. But he was also the general of the galleys and had in his time distinguished himself in many naval actions including the Battle of the Dardanelles. He had already proved his worth against the Turks at Candia and defeated them, and it was obvious that with the Pope so keen and obsessed to drive out the Turks from that place again, after they had recaptured it in 1669, Gregorio Carafa was considered to be the ideal person to do it. However, whether or not this was the case, the new grand master had many more problems to contend with before he could even think of mounting a naval operation against the Turks.

Although he was also a lover of art, Carafa felt he had to continue with Cotoner's unfinished works because of a sense of duty. So notwithstanding the fact that he had to fork out monies which the Order could ill afford and which could have been used for the naval operation the Pope wanted, he kept the services of Mattia Preti, and also continued with. The work his predecessor had started on fortifications and the

118

building of *Sarria* a small church on the outskirts of Valletta in the way of thanksgiving for the deliverance of Malta from the plague. Then in the same way as La Cassiere had built St John's Church and the other grand masters that followed kept making some artistic contribution to embellish this wonderful temple. The marble group showing the Baptism of Christ by St John the Baptist was originally commissioned by Grand Master Nicolas Cotoner from the Maltese artist Melchior Gafà. Unfortunately Gafà died suddenly and the project was shelved. It was during the reign of Grand Master Perellos that the work was now commissioned to the Italian artist Giuseppe Mazzuoli, who executed one of the most important and prestigious marble groups of the time.

It was in his time that the nuns in the Convent of St Ursula in Valletta who had been established by Grand Master Verdalle and endowed with both land and a share of the booty captured by the knights asked for a change in their status. The truth was that they had waxed fat and had become tired of watching from their screened roof the knights going out in their ships in search of booty to be captured, while they had to wait doing nothing to earn their share. So they asked for the privilege of supplementing their faith with work by participating in nursing activities with the knights. But Carafa refused their request telling them that while it was the men's lot to work, it was the women's duty to pray. They had then to accept their fate and submit to the grand master's revised rule which left them cloistered, receiving only their close relatives on visiting days, and doing this sitting modestly on benches, without gesturing, laughter, or gossip lest they lose their virtues and perfection.

Carafa's biggest problem however lay with his navy which the Order had as yet not tried to modify according to the times. Galleys were on their way out and sails were replacing oars in the new types of vessels. So although the Order's ships could still engage Barbary corsairs they could not hold their own against any big fleet like that of the Turks who were already changing their ships. The grand master found himself in a dilemma. He could either start rebuilding his fleet and forego expenditure on everything else, or if he were to maintain the order's levels in the fields of art, fortifications and standard of living engendered by the Renaissance, he would have to stick to what galleys he had and forego an attack on the Turks. He chose the latter and he might have been influenced in his decision when in 1683 the Order's navy was asked to fight for Austria, and then for Germany and Poland the year after. Carafa also helped the Venetians in their fight with the Turks in 1687, but besides proving to him that his navy could not be considered to be that obsolete, it also showed out his limitations.

The beauty of Valletta was enhanced when the grand master rebuilt the Auberge for the Italian Langue. This majestic building with his bust prominently displayed on the beautiful facade was to retain its importance for posterity. Today, after over 300 years it houses the Malta Tourism Authority. The passage of time had an even worse effect on the knights. Some of the stalwarts from the French and German Langues began leaving, many of them to fight against their brethren in the Wars of Religion. And although many of Europe's young Catholic aristocracy continued to join the Order in Malta these found little if any of the original noble scopes which had made the Order what it had been. With the approach of the eighteenth century then

The Grand Council chamber at the grand masters' palace, Valletta

new forces of disruption seemed to be more likely to complete the fragmentation of Christendom, something which had started with the Reformation. And this tended to turn the Order into a complete anachronism.

The statesmanship of Gregorio Carafa coupled with his dexterity for maritime affairs might have helped in some way to change the Order's history had he lived long enough. But he died in 1690 to be succeeded by the French Adrien de Wignacourt, a nephew of the previous Wignacourt. He is described to have been a zealous man, and to some extent also a lover of art. But that is where any resemblance to his uncle stopped. Truly enough it was during his reign that in 1693 an earthquake shook Malta for three days, causing much damage. The earthquake did a lot of damage to the Mdina medieval buildings, amongst which there was the old cathedral. Reputedly built over the remains of the house where St Publius, the governor of Malta, resided during the time when St Paul was shipwrecked. The cathedral was old and at least dated to the thirteenth century. Soon after the earthquake the cathedral chapter immediately set about planning a new church, and this was built to the designs of Lorenzo Gafà, the Maltese architect. It was completed in 1702. But his seven year reign served him only to continue with his predecessors' unfinished work with his showing neither the inclination nor the energy to divert the Order from its course which was leading towards its ignominious decline. The accent was of course on the obsolete navy which in those seven years had gone from bad to worse. It ceased to provide the incentive of adventure to the young knights, and these soon preferred doing their Caravans in French and Italian ports under the pretence of going there to obtain stores which of course they did, but only after finding relief in amusement they didn't find in Malta, and in agreeable female society. A stronger ruler had to be found, and first indications showed that Ramon Perellos y Roccaful, the Spaniard who was elected grand master to succeed Wignacourt in 1697 might have been the right man.

The new grand master was like his predecessors a lover of arts, but he was also a progressive and able administrator. He realized from the very start that his principal task was to try and revive the waning military prestige of the order, and this could only be done by bringing its fleet up to scratch and in line with the times. Nonetheless he had a more pressing commitment with St John's Church which he

A Flemish tapestry depicting the Nativity of Jesus commissioned by Grand Master Perellos

wanted to embellish with twenty-eight Flemish tapestries to be woven in Brussels from cartoons by Rubens. Being the wise man he was, the grand master wanted the by now ailing Mattia Preti to supervise the work so as to ensure their harmony with his own frescoes. Indeed his thoughtfulness paid, since Preti died in 1699 after having carried out his last assignment. And his mark can still be seen and appreciated till these very days in the tapestries that transformed the church into a precious galaxy of colour and ornamentation. Perellos also provided a set of tapestries to adorn what had come to be called the Tapestry Chamber in the palace of the grand masters in Valletta. Representing a profane medium which nonetheless is full of indescribable wealth and riot of detail, these Gobelins are the only surviving complete set of the series made from designs mainly Brazilian, as were presented to Louis XIV of France by Prince John Maurice of Nassau.

Perellos had started his reign at a time when nearly all the Christian nations of Europe for whose defence the Order always claimed to be organised, were making friendly treaties with the Turks in the interests of commercial prosperity. Moreover the knights now began to be restrained by France and Venice from approaching Eastern waters. Then the Holy See forbade them to interfere with the commerce of Greek and Jewish traders. This virtually left them with the only option of attacking Barbary corsairs. Then again these had become fewer and there could not be found enough booty to pay for the navy's upkeep. Were it not for its financial aspect this state of affairs might have been a blessing in disguise to provide the Order with time to change its ships. But it could not afford the expense at the time. On the other hand Perellos was convinced that the morale of his knights was deteriorating because of the waning prestige due to antiquated ships. And to set the ball rolling he decided to build the first of the new ships at his own private expense.

Strangely enough in his first attempt Perellos was inclined to revive the round-

Spinola Palace, St Julian's

bottomed Carrack type of vessel. At first his council did not agree, but after there was a poor show by the Order's galleys in a skirmish, he was allowed to have his own way. There was also at that time in 1700 the loss of the galley Capitana under the command of Bailiff Spinola. It was towing home a large galley captured from the enemy, but the Order's ship had been so damaged in the encounter that it foundered on the way with the loss of 500 men of her crew. Work was started on the first new ship which was to be called *San Raimondo*, after the grand master. Three others, the *San Giacomo*, *Santa Caterina* and *San Giovanni* were soon to be laid down as and when captured booty would enable the Order to pay for their construction. Then the system was adopted whereby two old galleys would be abandoned with every new ship that was built.

Even so, the knights were still far from reaping the same old harvests from raids on corsairs. The situation had been deteriorating for years, and it was calculated that in the previous 60 years the captured booty was only one hundredth of what was captured in the 60 years before those. Some of the missed money was being made up by Perellos by having the Order's ships help Spain to protect her African colonies and safeguarding Christian trade from pirates. It seemed for a time that the knights might have after all gone on the defensive. But there were soon to be a series of successful raids against the Turks. Perellos was so pleased, no doubt because this proved the continued usefulness of the navy, that he had a triumphal arch erected on the outskirts of Valletta which he named Portes des Bombes. Interesting more than the name of this arch is its motto in Latin – *Dum Thraces ubique pugno, in sede sic tuta consto*, meaning in English, 'Safely I am at home, while I fight the Turks everywhere'. The Order's navy also continued to produce the occasional powerful fighters of the kind of Romegas and Carafa of previous days, and this helped in no small way to counteract the common saying of those times that the Order had become smothered under wigs and powder.

One of the powerful seadogs who was virtually made up by Perellos was Jacques de Chambray. He had entered the Order at the age of thirteen as a pageboy, and he attended on Perellos when inaugurating the building of one of his new ships on which this Chambray eventually received his first training at sea. He did his first Caravan when the Order's ships went to the relief of the Spanish governor of Oran. But the best years of his service were done under Grand Master Vilhena and will be featured later on. However, after he retired from the service in 1749, he was appointed governor of Gozo. It was then that he devoted the rest of his time to fortify the small island, something which all the grand masters had failed to do. Indeed, throughout the first 200 years of the Order's stay in Malta, Gozo had always lain vulnerable to attacks by corsairs, with women and children more often than not being taken into slavery after a raid. Chambray built a fort with the help of his own private funds which he named after him. And the Gozitans could then take refuge there whenever there was a threat of a raid.

Grand Master Perellos died in 1720. This was a time when the Order could not afford to continue giving priority to the effects of the Renaissance. The eighteenth century brought forth other priorities. All Europe was affected. And so were the knights of Malta.

14

TRANSITION AND DECLINE

The first years of the eighteenth century marked the beginning of the age of the Grand Tour. Noblemen and gentlemen from the north of Europe began to descend upon the South, attracted by the changes brought over in the wake of the Renaissance. France and Italy were the biggest attractions. But Malta began also to have her share of visitors, all very keen for first hand information about the chivalrous knights and the island they had changed from a backwater into an epitome of Europe. Much as there was still a major part of the Maltese Islands, that was still bare and little better than a rock, this was amply made up for by Valletta the capital, Mdina and the three towns of Cottonera. The streets with their palaces, the picturesque forts and the magnificent churches that had by then been erected enthralled everyone. The ambience of the island spelt a story of achievement by the knights throughout their stay by then of almost 200 years, to be also considered as a prolongation of their previous time in Rhodes, and even of their first years at the times of the Crusades. But the centre piece of all the splendour was doubtlessly St John's Church by now enshrined with the glory of wealth and colour that the grand masters and knights of Malta had devised for it with their love of art.

Even so, the success of the knights in transferring Malta into the last Christian stronghold of Europe could be better seen through her people. There was history as evidence of how after long feudal occupations by various powers and races the Maltese when taken over by the knights in 1530 had almost all been simple peasants living a life of back breaking toil when not being harassed by corsairs.

But now they were transformed into a respectable community which notwithstanding the tradition of regarding of the knights as interlopers inherited from its forefathers, was now accepting these rulers and mixing with them to have better relations. This situation is to some extent confirmed by what Marchese Camillo Spreti, himself a knight, wrote in his Manuscript of a Knight of Malta in 1764 as edited by Averil Mackenzie-Grieve. Although being the prig he must have been, Spreti seems to have been prejudiced against the Maltese. He described the

St Anne's Chapel in Fort St Elmo with its coffered ceiling and intricately scupltured walls

Maltese/knights relations as follows: But the exclusive old Spanish families (referring to Maltese nobles) whose admission to the Order was forbidden, aloof in their dark palaces in the old walled capital of Notabile (Mdina) would have none of knight or Noble. The Barons are few and not tractable. Knights may be received only with the greatest difficulty into their houses, because having suffered various wrongs and discourteous treatment from the same, they do not wish to expose themselves again to similar affronts, and thus it came about that many Innocents must suffer from the bad behaviour of the guilty few. The counts entertain the knights more often, and among them are families in which one may spend a few hours pleasurably and without offence to God. The citizens who are either Clerks of the Order, or in some Public Service, or employed by the Treasury as Magistrates, Jurymen, Lawyers, Store-keepers, etc. are the ones who frequent such gatherings most, but here I do not advise you to go, not because they are lacking in honesty but for the reasons which I will give you. One frequents receptions firstly to learn and secondly to pass the time in honest diversions. If you go to these Citizens' houses for the first reason you will of truth be mistaken, for they understand little Italian and speak less. Although it is the foreign language mostly used by them, they do not know how to string together a serious well-salted conversation without using Arabic expressions which you will not be able to understand, and what is worse, in your presence they will often speak with another Maltese of the company in their own perfidious Idiom which is unknown to the knights, which shows as indeed their behaviour testifies in many other respects, little or no education. And you may be sure that when the Maltese talk in their own Idiom in your presence or that of other knights, they are criticising your appearance and your speech...

When it comes to women, Spreti brings out the wanted comparison himself when he first describes Maltese women at the time when the Order came to Malta in 1530 as 'having resembled proud and wayward savages, fleeing society and never permitting the knights to see their faces.' Then in his time he calls them predacious and perfidious, but the more dangerous for their great beauty which draws much attraction from the knights.

However, all the mentioned progress achieved by Malta and the Maltese by the eighteenth century admittedly attributed to the Order's rule, cannot in any way detract from the transition that had set in where the knights were concerned. As already mentioned this had started many years before. Now it gathered momentum, and it became clear that it was leading to the Order's decline. Spreti himself commented on this when he wrote that:

Behind the fascination of old observances of traditional ceremonies symbolizing a truly great past, behind the wealth and magnificence, there was decay. Boredom and Idleness, the Father of the Vices gripped the city gentlemen. Attached to their Auberges or Inns, the rich gay noblemen (the knights) perfunctorily performed their tasks and their often empty religious duties, using all their ingenuity and such energy as they possessed in devising fresh means of whiling away the appointed two years until they could become fully fledged knights and candidates for any of the Order's rich commanderies scattered throughout Catholic Europe. Gossip, gaming and duelling had again become their chief diversions; despite the vows of brotherly love which the Order professed, national rivalry throve between the knights of the various Langues...

The situation became paradoxical. While the Maltese seemed to have taken the road towards further improvement of their lot, the knights were sinking lower in their life of anarchism. Something had to be done to remedy the situation.

If there were those who were hoping for a good leader to resolve matters they must have breathed a sigh of relief when after Grand Master Marc' Antonio Zondadari who had succeeded Perellos, died after two years of reign in 1722, and the Portuguese Antonio Manoel de Vilhena was elected. Even though none knew what stock the new grand master was made of, his pale, refined and aesthetic features cut him out to be a good man, but his abilities had still to be seen. The truth was that they needn't have worried because Manoel, as he began to be known, was well aware of the hard task that lay before him, and he was not shirking the task.

There seems to be no doubt that one of his priorities was that of more accommodation for the people. The population had by that time increased to about 100,000, and habitation areas had become too small. This was what made him start with the construction of a residential suburb between the inner and outer lines of the Valletta fortifications. The planned town was to be called Subborgo Vilhena after him. Yet, the area had already been called Floriana, due to the fact that the line

The extensive lines of fortifications which enclose Valletta's suburb, Floriana

of fortifications had been built to the designs of the Italian architect Pietro Paolo Floriani.

It seemed however that the building of this town was only done in the way of a sideline for Vilhena's first attentions were also directed towards the revival of the Order's maritime power. Not in the way of ships, since the new building of these had been seen to by Perellos, but more in the way of action. Whether this was to be in the form of attacks on the Infidel in observance of the Order's motto, or attacking Barbary corsairs for booty to fill the Order's fast emptying coffers. There was also the other important scope of providing ways of Caravans for the young knights, and a distraction from sloth and laziness for the elders. This was by now thought by some to be the only way of solving the problem of decline. Indeed the knights wanted it, and so did the Pope who was also not happy with the future prospects of the Order.

Vilhena was still all out to oblige, and here he was fortunate in having not only the ships left by Perellos, but also, and what was more important, the right leader in the person of Chevalier Jacques de Chambray. This knight had in 1700 entered the Order as a page-boy at the age of thirteen in the time of Perellos. He had in fact attended to the grand master when he inaugurated the first of his set of new ships, and on which Chambray was soon to receive his first training at sea. When he became of age he went to France for some time but returned to Malta and joined the Order in 1706. He did his first Caravan when the Order's ships had gone to the relief of Oran. It was a trip wrought with fighting and pillaging during which the young Chambray was blooded and received his first wound. His courage and abilities immediately marked him for a meteoric rise in the service, and under Perellos he had his first promotion to lieutenant of the galleys. Now under Vilhena, in 1723, he was promoted captain of the *San Vincenzo* and from there he never looked back. He was destined to fight 31 battles and to capture 53 enemy vessels and to take booty to the amount of 1,500,000 livres. In fact by the time he came under Vilhena, in 1723, he had already acquired an international reputation. Because of his rubicund features, the Barbary Corsairs called him 'Le Rouge De Malte'. Spain also tried to induce him into her navy. But Chambray refused, and continued to serve the Order.

His most important achievement under Vilhena was when after a close four hour battle he captured the *Bellina* which was the vice-admiral of the Tripoli fleet. This victory shot his name even higher, as it also brought many positive reactions, the most important of which came from Pope Benedict XIII who in 1725 bestowed the honour on Grand Master Vilhena of the Stock and Pilier. The Stock was a casque of purple velvet adorned with the symbolic dove while the pilier was a sword with a lavishly ornamented pommel. No other grand master had as yet received that honour, and its significant importance could be inferred from the painting of the dead Philip II of Spain lying in state which can still be seen in the 'Maison du Roi' in Brussels, with the crown of Spain placed on the left of the body, and the Stock and Pilier on the right.

Chevalier Chambray used to boast that this honour was bestowed on the grand master because of the capture of the *Bellina*. But it was more likely that the Pope resorted to this award to rekindle the spark of heroism that appeared to be lacking in the knights, and which he believed could make them change their lassitude and general behaviour which was pushing the Order towards its decline. What's more, the Stock was more symbolic of peace than of war. Therefore it seems that the Pope had realised before anybody else that notwithstanding appearances, Grand Master Vilhena was more inclined to go by his time when the Acts of peace began to assert themselves over those of war.

Whatever was the real reason the award came at a time when the Maltese encouraged by support from the knights had become more enterprising in indulging in ceremonial festivities. They had never stopped taking part in the regatta held in Grand Harbour on the 8 September to commemorate the Great Siege of 1565, as they were also enthusiastic contestants of the Greasy Pole competition also held on that day. They still flocked in their thousands for the donkey races at Rabat just outside Mdina on the 29 June, the feast of St Peter and St Paul, as they also participated with zest in the Carnival organised by the knights. It was at this time too that in trying to emulate the initiative of Franciscan friars in Valletta who were the first to hold a procession on Good Friday so characteristic of a Passion Play with members of lay confraternities carrying life size statues of Christ's Passion, the people of Cottonera began to do the same. Many seamen from Vittoriosa, Cospicua and Senglea had seen such processions in Palenno and Spain from where they bought the artistic heads of Christ carved in gruesome realism of the various stages of His passion. They then made the bodies and pedestals in Malta, and also established the confraternities to hold the procession. At Vittoriosa this began to be held in 1725. In Cospicua and Senglea it began also at about the same time.

There were three days of festivities to celebrate the honour bestowed on the grand master. The Stock and Pilier together with the other gifts that accompanied them were exhibited in the church of St John for all to see and admire. The people loved Vilhena, and perhaps this could be seen through the posters that were stuck on the triumphal arches under which passed the Papal Envoy who had come to Malta to present him with the award. One of these read: 'Byzantium heard the name of the Order of St John, and trembled. Rome heard it and crowned it.' Another read: 'The Sovereign Pontiff Benedict XIII has armed the hand of the grand master with a sword to augment the terror of the Infidels and has adorned his head with a new majesty to augment the glory of the leader against whom the Infidels have fought.' Over the portals of the Magisterial Palace then there was a longer inscription which read:

Antonio Manoel de Vilhena
In whom Malta reveres a sovereign
The Order of Jerusalem a Grand Master;
    Rome a Hero;
Whose name fills the earth
Whose courage extends still further
Whom Nature has created for great deeds
Whom Faith has formed for the most courageous
Whom Virtue has elevated to the most glorious
Receives today from the Sovereign Pontiff Benedict XIII
The Sacred Hat, the Sacred Sword

✳   ✳   ✳

By the time Vilhena built the beautiful fortress on a small island that also bears his name in 1726 it came out that he might have after all been right. Now at peace with the Western nations, the Turks took a peaceful stance and there seemed to be no more scope for battles with the Order's fleet, as there was much less fear of an invasion.

Fort Manoel turned out to be a magnificent architectural achievement complete with a chapel dedicated to St Anthony, the patron saint of the grand master, with a testamentary clause to have a new gun installed every three years provided its commander was a Portuguese, and small things like that. It became more as a monument to its builder whose bust was placed over its handsome gate. But as a fortress it turned out to be a 'white elephant' and its guns were never fired in anger. But it signified an 'important transition in which Grand Master Vilhena began to consolidate the sovereign power of the Order through the arts of peace and what was even more important the centralisation of civil government.

In this last regard the grand master went out of his way to provide new seats for the Università, the commune of administration which had always been disregarded by previous grand masters and drew the complaints of the people. For the universitàs in Malta he built a most handsome palace, which is still used today by the Local

Vilhena Palace, Mdina

Council of Mdina. This building is attached to another baroque palace, the so-called Vilhena palace, today used as the National Museum of Natural History.

For the commune at Gozo he built the Banca Giuratale in the capital city of Victoria. If there was a sense of valour to be found in the grand master this was soon being manifested in his firmness when he swept away the traditional suzerainty of Spain in the affairs of Malta and removed the Spanish flag from the walls of Mdina (Notabile) where it had flown for over 400 years. Then when the viceroy of Sicily tried to re-assert his authority by sending a Royal Visitor to Malta, Vilhena stopped him from doing this and thus stopped once and for all the Order's dependence on old feudal relations. Even if he had to sacrifice the Order's Sicilian commanderies which were sequestrated as a means of retaliation. Vilhena was now also active with his intervention with Rome in the choice of a new Bishop for Malta.

It is also a fact that by his adroit consideration of the susceptibilities of the newer Maltese aristocracy, he raised hopes for old nobles that their status would be restored particularly where it concerned the eligibility of their offspring to join the Order on their own merits. Something which no other grand master had attempted to do.

There is no doubt that Vilhena's ways of transition were having the right effect on Malta, her people and the knights. Because he felt the need the grand master also built a house for poor women in the new upcoming town of Floriana, as he also found space and scope for the building of a hospital for incurables. But his greatest feat was achieved in 1731 when he built a theatre in Valletta which also took his name. Now the people of Malta were given the chance to enjoy and even educate themselves further by attending at the Masques, Comedies and other Divertissements performed and held at this theatre in which the eighteenth century delighted, with their always being crammed with thinly veiled complimentary allusions to the Magisterial virtues. Indeed Vilhena must have also found in this another way to occupy the knights, since notwithstanding that professional actors and musicians began to be brought from abroad to participate in the functions at the Manoel Theatre, the knights also played parts, particularly the Novices who were required to play the female parts. This beautiful theatre is considered as one of the oldest theatres of its time, which is still functioning till this very day, and functioning as it was intended to do by Vilhena.

Manoel Theatre, Valletta

But one cannot fail to appreciate the times when it served a better purpose with audiences made up of both knights and Maltese, arrayed in the brocades and perukes of the eighteenth century to see and enjoy some comedy of Goldoni or Moliere. All this thanks to Grand Master Vilhena, and of course the knights of Malta.

Had there ever been any doubt about Vilhena's chosen ways to rule the Order, these would have been settled in 1732 when Chevalier Jacques Chambray unexpectedly encountered the Muslim capital ship *Sultana* on the high seas and captured her. Vilhena didn't like it fearing it would disturb the state of peace prevailing then with Islam. But he couldn't blame Chambray since the Order's commitment to fight the Infidel had not changed. So Chambray was decorated with the grand cross for his efforts, as the grand master waited for any reaction. But there was none, and this action proved to be the last one of its kind. Indeed, after this incident there was a proposition by the Turks for a truce. Vilhena had lent a favourable ear, but somehow the proposal became abortive.

Vilhena was not destined to live long, but there was never a dull moment in his fourteen years as grand master. If he wasn't building he would find something to restore; if there was nothing wanting this, then it had to be something else. And his knights were kept busy. It might have been this attitude of his that made him turn his eyes on St John's Church, to which he had not donated anything to embellish it during his life time. Now he added two annexes to the Church providing additional ways of entrance from two principal streets of Valletta. As was to be expected then he completed his building programme by constructing his own country-house. This was nothing like the edifices constructed by some of his predecessors. It was just a genuine villa in Southern European style with its only exterior embellishments being four square-rumped stone lions, taken from his coat of arms, which also gave the building its name of Casa Leoni, meaning the House of the Lions. The interior was of course of a different aspect with spacious compartments all divided by ornamental arches topped by the grand master's shield of lion and winged sword, and enchanting vistas of orchards full of orange and tangerine trees, as well as other fruits whose

Fort Manoel, Manoel Island

fragrance when in blossom prevailed all over the place. It was a pleasant and a pleasing house, which was after all so characteristic of its owner.

When Grand Master Vilhena died in 1736 he was mourned by both the knights and the Maltese. All felt they had lost a leader and a friend who had devoted his reign to serve them and the Order he loved so much. He was to be remembered for posterity by the patrimony he left, and also by the impinging of his spirit on Fort Manoel to haunt it for a time, centuries after his death.

The haunting seems to have been connected with the chapel he had built at the fort, dedicated to his patron saint, St Anthony of Padua, which was eventually raised to the status of a Chaplaincy of Obedience and was still functioning as a church until 1942 when during World War II it was badly damaged during German air attacks on the fort, then being used by the British Navy. It was immediately after the end of that war that Captain Eric Brockman who commanded the fort set his men to clear the site of rubble in the hope of restoring some sense of order to the chapel. But from the moment of their starting work there was the appearance of a knight in black armour who at first terrified the men. But this spectre was neither violent nor in any other way malevolent and the men who saw him described the Black Knight, as he came to be called, as if he was supervising their work. This made them bold to get close enough to take a good look at his face, and descriptions that were given tallied closely to the features and armour of Grand Master Vilhena as they appeared in a portrait by Favray which still hangs in the grand masters' palace, now the President's palace in Valletta. All were then convinced that the ghost of the grand master was personally supervising their work as if he had an interest in what they were doing.

San Anton Palace, Attard

But more than for the restoration of the chapel, there was more concern to have some place where church services could be held, and this made Captain Brockman utilize the crypt beneath the chapel for this purpose. But when it was opened it was found that it had been entered by vandals. The altar and reliefs were wrecked, and paving stones covering graves were ripped up exposing human bones that from their medallions and inscriptions were identified to have belonged to knights of St John. It appeared then that this was the reason for the manifestation of the ghost and its attitude in urging the men with their efforts. As if the grand master was ensuring the restoring of the remains of his dead knights. So much so, that after the graves and crypt were restored, and masses said, the Black Knight disappeared and was never seen again.

This story was neither some figment of the imagination nor some traditional fabrication. It is authenticated by several persons who were involved. But even so there was a climax to this episode when in 1982 Captain Brockman then a civilian, informed me that even after so many years, the Black Knight was again haunting the fort. As this happened at the time when I was researching for my book *The Ghosts of Malta* I went myself to Fort Manoel where pitifully enough I found the chapel and its surroundings to be still in a dilapidated state, while the watchmen whose duties were to be at that place, were avoiding it because of ghosts. The climax came however when on going into the crypt which the Black Knight was haunting again, I found out that vandals had been into it anew, and the graves of the knights were again, open and with their contents exposed. This must have been what made the Black Knight or the spirit of Grand Master Vilhena haunt the place again.

133

The Portuguese Grand Master Manoel Pinto de Fonseca

15

THE LONG REIGN OF PINTO

The day came in 1741 when all roads led to Valletta, and the square in front of St John's Church had never seen so many people. The day had started by promising to be dull, but later the sun broke through of the clouds in a fiery splendour like a good omen and as if to 'complement the looks of expectation on every one's face in that ant-like crowd. Civilian clothing and black *faldettas* intermingled with the sombre black cassocks of priests and the powdered wigs of knights and the well-to-do, as the crowd pressed closer to the church with all eyes lifted towards the balcony over its portals.

They had all waited five years for that day. Since when after the death of Grand Master Vilhena everyone had hoped for and indeed expected a successor who would continue on his lines to lift the Order and the country from the pit of decadence into which it was falling. There had been all round disappointment when the Spanish Ramon Despuig was elected on that occasion, and time had proved that he was not the man to make an impact on the situation. Now, following his death, a new grand master was to be elected, and the crowds had gathered to hear his name being formally announced from the balcony of St John's as was always done. This time there was no disappointment, and when it was announced that the Portuguese Manoel Pinto de Fonseca was elected as the new grand master, the crowd shouted its approval and clapped, and went into an even greater frenzy of joy when Pinto himself appeared on the balcony to acknowledge the people's felicitations.

Grand Master Pinto made it quite clear from the very start that he proposed to carry on in the footsteps of Vilhena with the consolidation of the sovereign power of the Order through the arts of peace, and the centralization of government. Indeed it was believed that he was the one who could do it since he had served as vice-chancellor to Vilhena and had therefore very likely understudied him. However, much as he used the same wording as Vilhena, his ways were to be different. True enough he was soon spreading the word around that rather than using pike and gun, his favourite weapon to help progress and maintain peace would be diplomacy.

And there is no doubt that his statement was welcomed all over Europe, coming as it did at a time when the Austrian Succession War had become a very confused affair. Prussia, France, Spain and Bavaria were all fighting Maria Theresa of Austria, while England, Hanover, Holland and Savoy were all defending her, although each belligerent pursued his own way with little regard for the others. This state of affairs favoured Pinto since as will eventually be seen he was very much inclined for international showmanship, but it had to take second place to his start in ruling Malta and the Order.

His first move was evidently made in an endeavour to preserve the decorative pomp of the past. Like his predecessors, Pinto wanted to take possession of the cities of Mdina and Vittoriosa. It had become the custom that every newly elected grand master would agree with the local universitàs on a date and they would then go and take official possession of the two cities. The activities would be held on different days, and it was generally accepted that these would be occasions for great pomp and celebration.

Then after taking office he turned to tackle the first problem he had inherited from Despuig when he found that the financial situation of the Order was not that healthy. Indeed, unemployment was rife and he had to curtail it. So he had to resort to raising a loan. This made it possible for him to start a number of building projects. He started with the building of the new auberge of Castile and the Castellania in Valletta. He also constructed the lower part of Fort St Elmo, and there were many other projects going on. Meanwhile, the population of Qormi had requested the grand master to honour the village with the title of a city, and he obliged by honouring it with the title of Città Pinto.

Another autocratic move was made when he introduced the planting of mulberry trees and the cultivation of silkworms with the intention of laying the foundations for the silk industry. True enough, however well intended the scheme might have been, none was impressed. But the surprise came when Pinto struck a medal to commemorate the occasion for posterity. It was nothing in itself, but when medals continued to be struck to commemorate other simple occasions, it made people think. When Pagery and the College were improved, and printing was introduced there was a beautiful medal struck showing Minerva engaged in instructing fat little *putti* in geometric and typesetting, with the motto, *Regi Artium Restitori*. Even a simple decree to check the growing luxury of dress qualified for a medal this time showing moderation applying a torch to a heap of finery. To both the knights and the Maltese people it began to become evident that more than being keen to improve their lot, the grand master was obsessed in having posterity remember him as some thoroughly modem and enlightened ruler. Unless he was preparing the ground for something else.

Believing that he had made the desired impact in his home rule, Pinto turned to cultivate his international relations. Here it must be said that inconsistent with his pacific and progressive views, the grand master remained persistent with his feud with the Turks. Many historians attribute this to the knights' refusal to come to terms with the Infidel because of fanatical and medieval obsessions. I would say because any such arrangement would have been against their vows. And this was why the Pope as well, although not showing it, was against any such arrangement. But the Christian maritime countries with whom Pinto was now furthering relations, although having negotiated tolerant and amicable pacts with the Turks, and to all intents and purposes occasionally pressed Pinto to do the same, really preferred Pinto to remain adamant. This was because they were still sustained by the sense of fear the Order's fleet at Malta continued to inspire. Even though it was often being stated that this fleet could by then only irritate the Turks, it was still being considered as the traditional Police of the Mediterranean. Those countries, particularly France were playing a double game with Pinto. And he should have realized this and its dangers in 1748.

Well before then the knights had cause to be perturbed by the growing number of slaves they had in Malta. In January 1748 on the other hand a number of Christian slaves on a Turkish galleon mutinied and succeeded in overpowering the crew and took over the vessel while this was on a passage from Rhodes to Anatolia in Turkey. On 2 February they brought the captured vessel to Malta and the knights were overjoyed when they discovered that amongst the Turkish prisoners there was Mustapha, the Pasha of Rhodes. Being such an important prisoner he was put in comfortable quarters at Fort St Elmo and treated accordingly. But a few months later on learning of this capture, the king of France, because of his country's friendly relations with the Turks, asked Pinto to release the prisoner.

Without any further word, the grand master had the Pasha released in May 1749. The Turk thanked both Pinto and the King of France but preferred to remain in Malta where he was allowed to stay notwithstanding the indignation of the knights. Pinto thought he had won his point when the Pasha eventually took the Catholic faith and also married a Christian girl, and even the knights had to admit that their grand master might have been right after all in doing what he did. But the situation wasn't as innocent as it seemed because the Pasha indeed placed himself at the head of a dangerous plot. He employed one of his countrymen as his secretary and found ways and means to carry out secret correspondence with the Turks. A plot was hatched and it was timed to take place on the 29 June 1749 which was the feast of St Peter and St Paul traditionally known as *Imnarja*, when as the Pasha knew, most of the people in Valletta and the other towns would go to the feast and other celebrations held at Notabile. A trusted slave at the grand master's palace was entrusted to cut off Pinto's head, and then inform the slaves at the stables and the kitchen by throwing down a flower pot from the balcony. Those slaves then, all trusted and unencumbered, would disarm the guards and set all the other slaves free. They would enter the Armoury and take weapons and munitions to besiege Valletta until a Turkish fleet which would be waiting would land more troops, enough to capture the island.

All was set and the conspirators had only to wait for the day. Even some foreign guards at the palace were bribed by sums of money to collaborate. Had they stopped there with their preparations, the Turks would have certainly captured Malta.

Only that the secretary of Mustapha together with a Portuguese renegade tried to corrupt a Maltese soldier, Giacomo Cassar, while they were sitting in the coffee-shop of a Jew named Cohen. The Maltese refused to play up and also rebuked them for their attempt, which made the Turkish secretary lose his temper and slap the

Maltese soldier. Fearing a fight, Cohen drove the Turk and the Portuguese away from his shop, then he asked the Maltese what had happened. Cassar revealed the plot, and that was that. Both the Jew and the Maltese went separately to the grand master with the information. Now Pinto acted immediately. Both the Turkish secretary and the Portuguese renegade were arrested, and by the following morning were subjected to torture and revealed the names of 150 conspirators, they also mentioned that Mustapha Pasha was at the head of the plot.

Mustapha denied this, showing himself as being similarly surprised and expressing satisfaction that the culprits were under lock and key. But Pinto was not that foolish to believe him. Mustapha was arrested and well-guarded, also to protect him from the crowds of Maltese who tried to get at him at St Elmo. The grand master then wrote to the King of France telling him he was taking the necessary steps to inflict the necessary punishment. But the King disagreed and asked the grand master to release Mustapha and let him return to his country, which Pinto did. Thirty eight of the others were publicly hanged for the attempt. This went down into the annals of Maltese history as The Plot of the Slaves.

✻   ✻   ✻

The French reaction did not go unnoticed. But much as the knights were indignant (maybe with the exception of the French ones) Pinto did not say another word on the matter. Not because he was the servile person some might have made him out to be, but because he had other plans which made him avoid French antagonism. More than France he had Corsica in mind. The island which was much bigger than Malta and similar with mild winters, and where the mulberry and olive could thrive; and which was at that time already struggling to throw off the yoke of Genoa. Pinto was thinking of ways and means to annexe it to the Order's domains. There was to be no question of a war. His fleet was still not up to standard for that, and now in 1749 his top admiral Jacques de Chambray had retired from the service, and more to keep him in harness he had appointed him Governor of Gozo. It was during his time there that Chambray built the fort that still bears his name. The intention was to provide defence and refuge to the Gozitans during enemy raids. As things turned out Fort Chambray had never to endure any siege from Barbary corsairs, and its value was only a prophylactic one. Chevalier Chambray used 400,000 livres of his own money to build the fort.

In the meantime Pinto had already begun paying great sums of money to win Rome in helping him achieve the annexation which was his latest whim. Until the time came for him to make the move he continued with scoring what were considered to be small victories in the cause of peace, always making sure to strike a medal for the occasion. It was in this sense that he worked out an amicable settlement of the long standing feud the order had with Venice since the time of La Cassiere. There were also medals struck with nothing in particular to commemorate. One of these showed him rising majestically from his throne to receive a band of convert refugees from the Barbary states on whom the Holy Spirit poured its rays. Then as if to drive his point with France and Spain, anticipating their involvement in his eventual acquisition of

Corsica, he struck another medal showing squadrons of the Order saving a French galley on one side, and on the reverse showing them protecting Spain from the attacks of the Barbaresques. It seems that this question of medals had become more like a public relations exercise for Pinto, and one wonders whether after all this obsession of his had contributed to make Malta more cosmopolitan as it indeed became in those times.

The influx of more foreigners in the island for both business and pleasure must have brought a certain amount of laxity. But what concerns us here is the attitude of the knights. New ideals and ideologies had been stirring even during the first few years of Pinto's reign radiating new ways of thinking and behaviour, even though not always correct. But then there was now also the grand master showing a certain amount of libertinism which made it impossible for him to check similar behaviour amongst his knights. It was then already being whispered that the pandering of the Maltese to the knights which had set in by that time was done at the price of the morality of Maltese women. And Camillo Spreti who has already been quoted, wrote something to this effect in 1764. There was also the dubious association with bad characters and adventurers who roamed in cosmopolitan Malta in those days, and which the knights were duty bound to avoid both by statute and status. Yet, it was Pinto himself who broke this rule by associating with a notorious adventurer of those times. So positions were switched over, and instead of having the grand master watching over his knights, it befell to these to watch their leader and his doubtful behaviour.

First details about this strange association by Pinto emerge from a diary of one Ignazio Saverio Mifsud, a Maltese scholar, which is still preserved in the Malta Library. The particular entry under the date of 21 February 1754 reads as follows:

For some months there has been lodging in the palace of His Most Serene Highness a man who claims to be a chemist. This man was received by his aforementioned Highness and admitted to his full confidence, being lodged in his palace and maintained at his own expense. He occupied the rooms surrounding the loggia of the fountain made by His Highness in the Garden Court. And the reason of all this is that he had announced his intention to concoct a certain elixir of life designed to keep man sound in health both in body and mind.

It later transpired that this man was a vagabond who originally went by the name of Balsamo or Balsano but later calling himself Count Cagliostro. He spent his time imposing himself at one period or another on most of the great people of his day.

It was not known what made Pinto associate with this man or what he was doing during his stay at the grand masters palace. Although jokingly there were those who assumed that he might have been preparing one of his special elixirs, which seems to be supported by the fact that Pinto lived to the ripe old age of 92.

It seems that although Pinto must have known that his misdemeanours had become common knowledge in Malta and could push the Order further into decline rather than lifting it out as he had originally proposed, he was not perturbed. One good point that one must credit him with was that he was always trying to strike a balance, and when his influence was waning he would do something for the Order and Malta to make up. Even now when his popularity with both knights and Maltese was at an ebb he began the building of a Customs House and nineteen stores which were so badly required in those days as they are still very useful today more than 250 years later. For the Order he had other plans, but as he wanted the support of some powerful nation to execute them and did not want to use France or Spain for already known reasons, he diverted his attention towards Frederick II, King of Prussia, later known as Frederick the Great.

Pinto could not have chosen a better time. The Prussian monarch had become a ruler of great influence after seizing Silesia from Austria as he had also taken part in the partition of Poland. Being on the verge of the Seven Years' War and fearing that France would go against him, he was looking, round for a counter-alliance. Although the Order was not considered for this, Frederick could not help being impressed by Pinto's resistance to British pressure which was constantly growing for the use of Malta as a base. The grand master had continued to resist and in 1756 he did not think twice to impound the rudder of an English privateer that entered Grand Harbour without permission and imprison her captain. In the exchange of letters with George II, Pinto had addressed the monarch as 'Most Serene and Powerful King.' In turn, the English King addressed the grand master as 'Eminent Prince ... and beloved cousin and friend.'

But what might have made Frederick the Great even more amenable to make more friends, and the Order was not one to be ignored, was the fact that from 1750 to 1753 he had hosted the French philosopher Voltaire in Berlin from where he continued to radiate his modem philosophy challenging accepted beliefs and traditions thus preparing the way for the French revolution. Of course Pinto had not the slightest interest in the dissemination of such theories. All he wanted from the King was to use his influence to have the agents which the Order had always kept at the principal European Courts dignified with the title of Ambassador equivalent to that of other countries. This was granted, and now even Pope Benedict XIV granted the use of the Sala Regis at the Vatican to Ambassadors of the Order. On the strength of the new relations that were forged with the Holy See by Pinto on this occasion, the Pope also granted the use of the mozetta and cappa magna to the chapter of St John's Church. As was to be expected, Pinto struck another medal to commemorate the two occasions, this time showing a mounted ambassador passing under a triumphal arch.

The first Ambassador Extraordinary appointed by Pinto to enjoy the new honour was Bailiff Fra Laure de Breteuil who was appointed Ambassador in Rome. His arrival in Rome in 1759 for the presentation of credentials was a ceremony which must have warmed the cockles of the grand master's heart. The processional retinue was made up of 82 Mutes, two postillions and a courier, two trumpeteers and flag-bearers in blue and yellow vests with the arms of the Order in silver. He was then accompanied by Cardinal Portocarrero and Cardinal Secretary Rezzonico. Behind them then trailed a cavalcade of horses, baggage wagons, other postilions and a host of more horsemen with the Order's arms on their saddles.

Notwithstanding that it had taxed little if any of his efforts, none can deny Pinto the credit for this achievement which raised the name and prestige of the Order, and this when it was so badly needed. It also came at the right time to counter-balance the checking and refusal by the French of the grand master's aspirations for the acquisition of Corsica, making him also aware of the double-play behind their show of friendship. It could have also been considered as a fitting end of the colourful albeit tempestuous rule of the grand master, now eighty years old. But Pinto would have been the last one to agree with this. On the contrary he was convinced that his age, in particular the last few years with the many international contacts he had all over Europe, had opened his mind wider, and even made him change his outlook of his future reigning years. It was with this premise that he turned to devote his full attention to the Order in Malta, the people and his knights. As if in search of what further successes he had failed to obtain from abroad. And to maximise his sovereign authority in Malta in line with his new outlook.

Pinto was now seeing his as having become a materialistic age. In the sixteenth century, he began thinking, men had been willing to lay down their lives for religion, but in the eighteenth century all such excitement had died down. He felt that people were no longer interested in abstract ideas as in practical things, especially the good things of life. Indeed he knew of those who still boasted of the liberty of their government, as he had many a time done himself, but he had come to realize that the upper classes who controlled it neither expected nor desired that political power should ever be changed by humbler folk – nor did the humbler folk themselves aspire to it. He reasoned that his had become the golden age of privilege – the rich man in his castle, the poor man at his gate, and men regarded this as a definite and permanent state of things. It seemed to Pinto that civilization had arrived and that politics were henceforth to be merely the rivalry of groups of well-bred gentlemen who were divided more by personal connections than by earnest convictions. And in such a settled and ordered system, he concluded, it seemed to be vulgar to get excited or enthusiastic about anything.

Whether it was correct or not, this philosophy of Pinto, was to be reflected in the remaining turbulent years of his reign.

It was a new Pinto that in 1760 took stock of the situation in Malta and the Order. If he was old in age he was still feeling young in heart and spirit. As he was also feeling the hurried urge to reform the local situation in his own way. He could never forget that after all he was a prince, as he had always lived like one. But now he was also feeling like a fine-tuned engine racing at high revs to start reigning as the absolute ruler with overall authority even with the power over life and death.

It is true that the grand master had such over-riding powers. Whether he used them or not was another matter. But besides his enlightenment with the new philosophical thought it could have been the double face dealing of France that was now bringing the tyrant out of him. If indeed it were so then the incident of the Corona Ottomana which occurred at this time must have even showered more fiery embers onto the powder keg. This was a Turkish galleon which in 1760 had appeared off Malta with the obvious intent of entering Grand Harbour. As there were no signs of any aggressive activity on board, the gunners of Forts St Elmo and Ricasoli withheld their defensive fire, until it was soon discovered that the Turkish vessel was manned by Christians. It was the same old story of Christian slaves, amongst them some Maltese having overpowered their guards, and brought the ship to Malta. It brought back memories to Pinto of a similar incident in 1748 during which there was captured Mustapha Pasha who had eventually plotted the rising of the slaves. On that occasion the King of France had asked Pinto to release the Pasha. Now, he intervened again and ordered the grand master to return the captured vessel to the Turks.

For the third time Pinto had to eat humble pie from the French, and being what he was, and the state he was in, some sort of explosion was not excluded. It makes one wonder therefore whether it was coincidence that made the grand master set to rebuild the Auberge de Castile which belonged to the Langue of Castille, Leon and Portugal before starting on his general reform. It was the normal thing for each particular Langue to decide, build or remodel their auberges, but in this case, notwithstanding that there might not have been the need, and that the military ardour of the Order had declined, Pinto went ahead to rebuild the place. And what was more important, this time ensuring that his own family coat of arms give the keynote of the decorative scheme. Then giving the place a magnificent portal approached by an imposing flight of steps and surmounted by trophies, banners, drums, shields, spears and anchors; completed of course with his bronze bust in the middle. At the same time in 1764, the grand master was showing his mettle with Britain in a dispute concerning the Consul Dodsworth. He was the English consul in Malta, and a thorn in the Order's side. When Pinto imprisoned him there arose a diplomatic incident which brought a British protest. This was delivered to Pinto by Captain Harrison in the frigate *Centurion* which was what the grand master insisted upon before releasing the Englishman.

A seemingly revitalized Pinto now turned to the proper enforcement of his sovereign authority over Malta. Such authority is normally exercised in various ways, one being in the issue of coins. In fact the right to issue money had always been the privilege of a sovereign state. It was given as such to the first grand master in Malta L'Isle-Adam. Juan de Homedes then followed suit, but went a step further when for the first time he printed his own coat of – arms on the money he minted. And so did de Valette. Verdalle then had put the Cardinal's hat on his coins, while Wignacourt adopted the ducal crown. When issuing his own money, Pinto made sure that he would mint more than his predecessors had done, and that all were to bear his aggressive profile.

Now in his spurt of newly found energy, Pinto also arbitrarily set the value of the Spanish doubloon, the Sicilian Ounce, the Venetian, Portuguese, French, Roman, Florentine and Hungarian moneys in terms of Maltese scudi, tari and grani, also printing a table of values for use by merchants. In 1765 then he went ahead with issuing a decree ordering all payments of debts in foreign money to be effected by such rates.

None can of course today question Pinto's decree, but there must have been something wrong since it was very unpopular, and most of the complaints it raised were about the new coinage which he issued. It was alleged that coins were light of weight, and that the alloy that went into them reduced their value to one quarter of what it was meant to be. If this was true, then this could have been a case of open corruption.

The grand master was not bothered. Guided by his power which gave him full civil and criminal jurisdiction he could do as he pleased, and rule as he thought fit even though he was not always correct. It was on this same principle that at the same time he began to effect serious changes in legislation which were to have far reaching effects on Malta and the future of the Order. He reasoned that the control of civil powers had been illogical and unworkable from the very start. He considered that supervision of the Council by a body of elderly bailiffs who lived on their European commanderies had only a prejudiced effect: 'If I were king,' said Pinto, 'I would never assemble such councils. These gatherings almost always end by destroying the rights of those who would have permitted them to meet.' He might have been right, and none would have blamed him if he changed the legislation. But what he did was to abolish such council meetings, and thus the chapter general of the Order became absolute.

He had shorn the Giurati which had formed this parliament of the few duties that had been left to them. But in his characteristic way of striking a balance he had re-modelled their splendid Castellania in Valletta where although powerless, they could still in pompous robes of black damask and velvet, make a feint of administering civil justice. The post of captain of the Verga or Hakem as he was called was retained. How could he remove such a colourful and historic cog in the wheel of Maltese autocracy? But under the new rules, although the holder of the post was still to be chosen from the island's aristocracy, he was not to be elective any longer. All his functions were removed and all he had to do henceforth was to participate in ceremonials by standing at the grand master's right attended by a Page who will bear his Verga or rod of office.

The aristocracy had always been a headache for the Order. Since L'Isle-Adam the nobles had cultivated certain antagonism towards the knights, largely because of their not being allowed to join the Order. Pinto knew this, as he also knew how some of them managed to surpass this difficulty. He was also aware that Vilhena had tried to solve this problem and attained some success when he gave out some titles himself. This gave him one of his brilliant ideas, and he began to bestow titles freely, mostly on people from the middle class, which he followed up by encouraging social relations between the knights and leading Maltese families. When he saw that this was not going to work he went further with another arrangement for the knights whereby they could choose their own circle of friends and localities to frequent thus securing means of relaxation. This served Pinto as well in that it flattered the vanity of ambitious newcomers into the class of nobles.

It needs not be said that the Maltese resented these latest moves. As Camillo Spreti had occasion to mention in his manuscript of 1764, Grand Master Pinto had by this legislation robbed them of the last of their civic rights and liberties. And this tended to rub off all the good that he had done during his grand mastership. Because it could not be denied that beneath his showmanship, greediness and libertinism he had been a good grand master and an excellent administrator with his shrewdness and cunning always standing him in good stead when fighting for what he considered to be his right. And he might have also got away with this latest unwelcome reform had he not become inclined to turn a blind eye to the close and less legitimate association of the knights following his latest arrangement. It was this that made the people become even more glamorous.

In his by now characteristic way Pinto did not for a moment consider retracting and stuck to his guns. However, he could now see and feel the crumbling of the Order's foundations which he had tried and almost succeeded to bolster. He had to do something, and it was now that he turned to the Church which was sustaining the people's views. He could not touch the Bishop, and much less the Inquisitor. Censoring the knights for their conduct fell within their competence. But it was a different case with the Jesuits.

The knights had never seen eye to eye with these since their very first days in Malta. There had been the first dispute with Bishop Gargallo about the locality of the college he built for their order, but then over time there had been their interference when as confessors of various grand masters and senior knights they had become too influential in the Convent. In this case too they had come out on the people's side, and if he was to do it, he had to act fast. It was a very daring move he was contemplating, possibly the most daring one of his reign, and under different circumstances he might have thought twice about it. But there had also been the question of the fat holdings of Bishop Gargallo's Jesuit College. Pinto's greed had for a long time been tickling him to find ways and means of how to take them for himself. And it now appeared to him that his chance had come, and he could not let it go.

There was only one further difficulty in his way. It was only the Pope who could remove the Jesuits from Malta, and his friend Benedict XIV had since died and was succeeded by Clement XIV. So Pinto did not feel that easy to go to him with his request. He surmounted this by telling the Pope it was his 'suzerain' King Frederick II who was demanding the expulsion of the Jesuits from Malta. Rome knew well enough of Pinto's fabrication, but nonetheless the request was eventually granted, and the Jesuits were expelled from Malta in 1768. This immediately made the Inquisitor pounce on the Jesuits' college which he wanted to have added to his domains. And this in turn brought Pinto roaring into battle for what he wanted for himself.

It was a big fight. When the Pope himself ordered Pinto to hand over the property of the exiled Jesuits to the Inquisitor, the grand master refused. In an endeavour to resolve the deadlock then the Pope consented to the building being passed to the University of Studies Pinto wanted to establish. It could be that this was Pinto's last resort to oust the Inquisitor after seeing that his was a lost case. But whatever it was, the Pope decided the issue and as a result Malta had her University on the foundations of the suppressed Jesuits' College in Valletta, which was eventually conferring degrees in the various faculties, and render service to Malta.

This might have also been considered as another way of striking a balance. As if establishing a University to make up for the loss of civic rights and liberties and the other laxities that went with them. But if Pinto thought so, this time he was wrong. For much as the establishment of a University might have been appreciated, the situation had become one that for the first time in the history of the knights of Malta, whilst clamouring for the return of their rights, people were also whispering to each other – that the grand master must go.

16

SEED OF REBELLION

The Seven Years War (1756–63) fought by Britain and Prussia against France and Austria had practically eliminated the Order from the international limelight. The knights must have tried to revive the issue through drama they organised in Malta with great sounding long themes about the grand master's policy of ruling through peace. One such drama bore the title of 'How war frenzy existed in Europe with such harm to the human race.' Another title that featured in Le Belliche Contingenzi d'Europa (Serenata 1760) was 'War is by nature boastful and devastating with its events being always injurious to both victors and conquered, consisting in terror and cruelty.' Now, in 1769 there was also a *Componimento* dedicated to Grand Master Pinto wherein the interlocutors were Jove, Mars and Minerva. Showing to what depths the Gods of War had sunk in the eighteenth century. But nothing of these was bound to re-attract international attention, as the knights seemed to be trying to do.

However, there was one interesting approach from Russia. It must be said that this country had originally established relations with the Order at the time of Peter the Great who in his time considered Malta as a possible valuable base for his operations against the Turks. Now Empress Catherine II, sent Pinto a state portrait by Levinsky as a gift, which still hangs in the grand masters' palace. It was then not difficult for the Empress to charm the old grand master to help her in building up her infant navy. He first allowed her officers to train in ships of the Order, and then later even sent two of his bailiffs to reorganise her Baltic fleet for the war with Sweden.

The Russian Empress was an intelligent, cultivated and autocratic ruler who marked her reign by imperialist expansion and extension of serfdom. It seems that Pinto did not realise what might have been behind her new friendly relations.

One international development which the knights did not fail to attract to Malta was that of literature about new ideas by Voltaire and also by the other political philosopher Rousseau, whose main work of political theory *Le Contrat Social* based on the theme that 'Man is born free and everywhere he is in chains' began to radiate new ideas. These now also reached Malta and began to stimulate new beliefs in some of the knights, particularly the French. The younger knights then were for the first time hearing of the Rights of Man, and it was obvious that they would try to reconcile these with the trends of their society.

This was another subversive wave the old Pinto had to contend with and combat if he was to resist the decadence that had by now begun to set in the Order. It is very likely too that these new teachings had already swayed some of the knights on to the side of the Maltese who had continued to resent the grand master's arbitrary withdrawal of their civic rights. So much so that there were knights who not only began to champion the Maltese cause, but were even implying hopes of succeeding Pinto on his death, so as to return all the rights he had withdrawn to the Maltese people.

But it appeared as if Pinto was still far away from dying. Notwithstanding his old age he was still not infirm and continued to give his personal attention to all matters of state, as well as to his private affairs whether lawful or clandestine, particularly where these concerned monetary gain. It was at this time that it became known how he had scandalously taken money which rightly belonged to the Archconfraternity of the Souls of Purgatory, one of the religious societies that were often sprouting up. This one, which was based, as it still is, in Valletta, used its monies for the saying of masses and other services for the repose of the souls in purgatory.

If one were to look for one instance where Pinto might have shown that he was losing his grip this could have been in the need for storage of documents. He was aware of the historical treasure in the form of documents and books that had accumulated throughout the two hundred and forty years of the Order's rule in Malta. Thousands of records with which the organisation was concerned both in Malta and in its properties and commanderies in every country in Christendom. To these there were added the 7,900 volumes given by Bailiff Louis Guerin de Tencin in 1763. All of these lying unclassified and without a semblance of any order at the place used as a library at St John's Church. It was something to preoccupy the grand master, and he felt and was indeed very much concerned about building a proper library on the lines of other buildings with which he and his predecessors had embellished Valletta to take all this precious material and preserve it for posterity. He planned such a building. But he did not proceed with it. It was either that the Order did not have the necessary money, or that he knew he would not live to see it completed. But if indeed it were so, and Pinto could feel the approaching end, he certainly did not want to admit, and much less show it.

Patrick Brydone who published a book about *A Tour through Sicily and Malta* in 1773 had this to say of his meeting with Pinto on 6 June 1770.

The palace is a noble though a plain structure, and the grand master (who studies convenience more than magnificence) is more comfortably and commodiously lodged than any prince in Europe, the king of Sardinia perhaps only excepted. The great stair is the easiest and the best I ever saw ...

He (the grand master) has now been at the head of this singular little state for upwards of thirty years. He received us with great politeness, and was highly pleased to find that some of us had been in Portugal. He mentioned the intimate commercial

146

connections that had so long existed between our nations and expressed his desire of being of service to us, and of rendering our stay in his island as agreeable as possible.

He is a clear-headed, sensible little old man; which at so advanced a period of life, is very uncommon. Although he is considerably upwards of ninety, he retains all the faculties of his mind in perfection. He has no minister but manages everything himself; and has immediate information of the minutest occurrences. He walks up and down stairs, and even to church, without assistance; and has the appearance as if he would live for many more years. His household attendance and court are all very princely; and as a grand master of Malta, he is more absolute, and possesses more power than most sovereign princes.

Patrick Brydone also commented as follows about the knights he met whilst in Malta.

All the knights and commanders have much the appearance of gentlemen and men of the world. We met with no character in extreme. The ridicules and prejudices of every particular nation are by degrees softened and worn off by the familiar intercourse and collusion with each other. It is curious to observe the effect it produces upon the various people that compose this little medley. The French skip, the German strut, and the Spanish stalk, are all mingled together in such small proportions, that none of them are striking; yet every one of these nations still retain something of their original characteristic: It is only the exuberance of it that is worn off.

In another part of his book while dubbing Pinto as the Prince who aped the sins of monarchs as well as their splendour, Brydone mentions the tears and lamentations of the knights' mistresses as these gathered on the bastions to wave farewell to their lovers as their ships departed on an operation against Turks. This must have been a little farfetched since other evidence strikes one as if at the time of Brydone's visit, the grand master and the knights had reached a status quo in history – with Pinto trying to hold to dear life and the status he reached and cherished, while the knights were biding time until they could find a successor. Not included in this picture there were of course the Maltese, who had not stopped feeling, since they had been deprived of their rights, that Pinto must go.

The expected outcome came in 1773 with Pinto, now 92, being the protagonist till the very end, also showing his sangfroid on his death-bed. When the priest who was assisting him in his last moments asked him to rectify his lapse when he had defrauded the Confraternity of the Souls in Purgatory the ailing Pinto replied, 'Don't bother father, I will soon be meeting those souls, and I will explain all to them.' This must have been his last act of defiance in life, for soon after he died; unwept, uncoloured and unsung.

*　　　*　　　*

The Spanish Francisco Ximenes de Texada had been one of the knights who had sided with the Maltese during Pinto's tempestuous internal revolution. He had also spoken in favour of rescinding the harsh legislation Pinto had made. But when he was elected grand master to succeed him he might not have after all been happy about it. In truth the people welcomed him. Maybe in the sense that anyone could be better than Pinto. The knights too had seen him as one of those who could stop the people from revolt. Then more likely to encourage him in his new hard task, rather than because of merit, the Pope, now Clement XIV awarded him the Stock and Pilier as had been done to Vilhena. This still did not make his task easier.

Looking around him Ximenes found various tasks he had to carry out, but all of them requiring funds which were lacking. Even if it was to make some sort of a start he had the Monte di Pietà which was the Government pawnbroking department established in the sixteenth century, newly housed in a handsome building in Valletta, where it still is today. In the first few months of his reign then, a problem had cropped up with imported wheat that had increased in price. And before he could consider any measure of relief in the constitution, which the Maltese people were waiting for, he knew he could not avoid having to increase the price of wheat to the consumer, which automatically meant an increase in the price of bread which was the mainstay food of the Maltese, both rich and poor. He delayed a few weeks in taking a decision, possibly also cursing Pinto for having abolished meetings of the council of the chapter general which would in such case have shouldered responsibility. But he must have also appreciated his predecessor's way of taking a quick decision even when this was likely to raise public complaints.

When he increased the price of wheat there was uproar. But somehow, albeit with much difficulty, Ximenes kept calm. To the people it appeared as if he was not the good and understanding person they had thought he was. But to him it meant confirmation that he had to use an iron hand if he was to rule. And from that day what restless temperament had been hidden in him all came out, with his quick plunges from argument to black despair now beginning to keep also his knights in a state of constant apprehension. And this had him stamped as a despot.

To be fair it must be said that Ximenes did not tire in trying to reverse the Order's by now fast decline. But the situation in Europe had in his time become even more complicated. With Britain being involved in the quarrel with the colonies, there was also trouble brewing which eventually was to lead to the War of American Independence in which France and Spain joined against the British. Even Russia and Prussia had their hands full in trying to resist the British Navy's practice of preventing neutral merchantmen from supplying the enemy with goods that might be used for the promotion of war. This left little if any scope for the furtherance of relations with the Order which was now also at its lowest ebb. The situation also became such that with the increased incursions of the fleets of large nations in the Mediterranean, even the raids against Barbary corsairs had become more scarce and difficult, with this business of course becoming less lucrative. As described by a traveller to Malta in those days, the once dreaded fleet of the knights could be seen in Grand Harbour superbly ornamented as always, with gold blazing on the ships' numerous bas-reliefs and carving on the stem, as well as the enormous sails striped blue and red, to render a magnificent spectacle as if they were kept more as an emblem of their ancient splendour than for practical purposes. Once they served to render the Order illustrious; but now they only attested selfishness and decay.

This more than anything else reduced the takings from booty which made Ximenes look elsewhere for much needed funds. It was then that he felt himself forced to lower salaries of Government employees and this brought even more protests from the population. All such protests and clamours were all being transmitted to the grand master by the Church which by now began to take a more active part in defending the people. With Bishop Pellerano becoming the grand master's main opponent.

It was following such protests that the grand master was struck by an idea aimed to increase the local food supply by restocking the island with game. So he forbade the shooting of rabbits for a certain period. The Bishop, by now always on the alert to resist what was considered to be unreasonable legislation, immediately complained. His argument was that as rabbits tend to destroy crops, their preservation and increase would eventually provoke a famine, rather than more food. Ximenes relented, but only to compromise by relaxing the law in favour of Episcopal lands, until he discovered that the Bishop interpreted this concession as the right to kill rabbits for himself and his canons and other members of the clergy as well as the not so small number of tonsured 'clerks'.

Ximenes had hardly been a grand master for a year when such disputes began arising so often that they left him little time for other things. Many of them, admittedly, involved petty matters, but they were always being maximised by the clergy who were now taking after their Bishop and not losing any opportunity to complain on behalf of the people. This annoyed Ximenes so much that he did not think twice in reacting by interfering with the privileges of the clergy. With these together with the people being incensed as they were with his handling of the situation, his was the hair that broke the camel's back. Strong petitions were made to the King of Naples, informing him of the conditions that were flagrantly being imposed by the Order, and asking for steps to be taken to have them revoked. Being even impatient to wait for replies, the more zealous members of the clergy decided on a rebellion. It was not that difficult to persuade the people, and it was one of the most zealous priests, Don Gaetano Mannarino that placed himself to lead the uprising.

On the night of 9 September 1775 some of the rebels, after obtaining false keys entered St James Cavalier in Valletta, while others entered and took hold of Fort St Elmo. Then the city gates were opened to allow in the crowds that had been prompted to assemble there and go into Valletta to assist the rebellion. But to the ringleaders' surprise the crowd they found there was much less than they had expected. Obviously many had not found the courage to comply with the orders given, presumably fearing the Order's punishment in the way of retaliation.

But the most surprised man was Ximenes himself. He had never expected the Maltese to revolt against him. The more so that they had never done it against any other grand master. He immediately sent knights and soldiers to St James Cavalier where it was found that there were only four men holding the place, and these quickly surrendered. It was a different story at St Elmo where the rebels were still in possession of the fort on the following day. It was the Bishop, who feeling his responsibility in the matter urged them to offer to surrender if the grand master promised to restore the people's privileges as he had promised to do at his election. An envoy was therefore sent to Ximenes with the offer, adding that the rebels were also to be allowed to leave the fort unmolested.

The grand master accepted the offer right away and the situation was soon returned to normal. For a few days it seemed as if all had quietened down and notwithstanding the shortcomings, the people were considering that they had scored a victory and would soon be getting their lost rights back. But Ximenes had no intention of doing this, and instead he had the ringleaders arrested while a few days later the heads of three of them were impaled on the gates of St James Cavalier. Don Gaetano Mannarino was condemned to imprisonment.

As was to be expected this triggered the people again into rebellion, and this time there was to be neither fear nor lack of response. The Maltese rallied in their thousands behind new ringleaders and the Order had never faced any such danger which could finish by throwing them out of Malta. Ximenes might not have been so worried, but the knights were. They had themselves condemned what their grand master had done and now they openly threw their lot with the Maltese. Not to fight or use any weapons, but to calm them and promise them their support in the matters at issue. Although the revolt was somehow further delayed, but the knights' genuine attempts did not stop it. It was fate that did, when Ximenes died before that year was out. Whether or not the trouble he had to go through had caused his death is not known. But even though the rebellion had been nipped in the bud, it had served its purpose to draw the sympathy of the knights. They were now more than ever before wanting to cultivate their friendship with the Maltese, in anticipation of the tide that was threatening Europe which could very well also hit the Order adversely. The lack of love for Grand Master Ximenes was then marked for posterity when in contrast with the decorative memorials on the graves of other grand masters in the crypt of St John's, that of Ximenes was only given a soft stone tablet with his name.

17

A LULL BEFORE THE STORM

Whatever good intentions the knights of Malta might have had after the demise of Ximenes, nothing was going to change the fact that they had already decayed fatally. And time could not be moved back. Moreover there was now the new situation in Europe that they had to contend with.

The distinction between social classes in the eighteenth century meant much more than it does today. The upper and lower classes seemed to inhabit different worlds making it almost impossible for a man born in humble circumstances to cross the barrier between them. In France, Germany and Spain the aristocracy had clung tenaciously to the privileges enjoyed by its class. Britain too, although less rigidly, had followed suit. As an example one can mention that it was almost impossible for anyone not of aristocratic blood to hold a military commission in those countries. As all persons of noble birth like the knights were, expected to be exempted from the most onerous of taxes, thus throwing the heaviest burden of taxation on to those least able to bear it. For a time it had been felt that sooner or later there had to be a reaction against such monstrously artificial order of society, as if to emphasize that as all men were equal in the eyes of God, they should also be similarly equal in the eyes of the law.

As has already been indicated this kind of reaction had started in France during the latter half of the eighteenth century. And fired by the theories of Voltaire and Rousseau had spread all over Europe, including to some extent also Malta. It was a situation that was not going to be bettered by the knights' life of wigs and powder or their white-gloved ceremonial. It had also found them unprepared with their soft living and continued quarrelling over miniscule points of precedence that did nothing but make them have to kill time which in those fast moving days had for them become the worst of murderers.

This was the kind of situation inherited by the newly elected grand master in 1775, Emmanuel de Rohan-Polduc. He was a French aristocrat of the first order. But he was also a friendly cultivated person who made it a point to keep abreast of the fast changing times, in particular where these concerned science and economics. He was of course well aware of the new dangers to the Order which he was duty bound and indeed more than determined to counteract. But he also felt that his first priorities were to reconcile the feelings of the Maltese people to their rulers if he were to count on public cooperation in the approaching turbulence. The first thing he did on being elected was to have removed from the bastions the heads of the conspirators that Ximenes had impaled there. And that was not just intended as an introductory move, because he was by nature also a humane man. So much so that he did not take long to abolish torture altogether.

These might have been two welcome moves which spelt a good omen for relations with the people in the future. But the grand master was soon setting the ball rolling for a legal reform which was eventually to lay down the Code Rohan that was to form the basis of the common law in Malta together with the Codex of Justerin still operative in these times.

How about the knights? Did they play up with their grand master's new image and his peaceful reign? Not quite. In particular those of the three French Langues who more than ever before had become more conscious of what they considered their super strain. In fact this soon came to a head when a contested election to the coveted office of prior to St John's Church who was one of the higher dignitaries of the Order took place, and a Maltese, Fra Albino Menville was elected notwithstanding the heavy opposition from the three French Langues wanting to elect their French candidate. When the Maltese was eventually confirmed by the Council for the post, the French knights objected and went even so far as to insult the new prior at his installation. There was immediate reaction from the Maltese people who would have attacked the French knights were it not for the right and timely intervention of the grand master.

This served to show De Rohan what he might have to contend with in the future even from his compatriot knights who after their preoccupation at the despotic behaviour of Ximenes seemed to have become more rude and quarrelsome themselves as if oblivious to the approaching hard times. It seems that in contrast to their good grand master who was all out pulling all ropes in an effort to save the Order, the knights of Malta were now determined to push it into the scrap yard of history.

Even so, the good De Rohan might have had the interests of his knights in mind when in 1789 there was established the Anglo-Bavarian Langue. This was the creation of the new Bavarian knights, who were placed within the dormant English Langue. Thus, the Order obtained land and at the same time retained the 8 languages. For the newly established Langue, there was given to them a palace that was erected near the end of the seventeenth century, to be known as the Auberge of Baviere. He then became the first grand master to admit women to his receptions, while he gave his patronage to Żebbug which had asked the grand master to elevate their status to that of a city, as had happened with Qormi. The grand master accepted their petition and gave them the title of Città Rohan. He also spared some thoughts for defence when he supported the building of Fort Tignè. This was built at Dragut Point, called so as there was a battery placed there on the instructions of the famous pirate, Dragut.

In the time of Pinto there had already been some whispering about the formation of a Masonic Lodge in Malta. Now this came into the open and indeed fashionable immediately after the combination of the Anglo Bavarian Langue. Two years later in 1785, a Bohemian Count Kolloviath visited Malta with special letters for the grand master. And this seems to have given more popularity to the Lodge. So much so that the grand master himself eventually became a member. Subsequently the Lodge had to tone down its activities after a woman went to her confessor with a story of orgies that were taking place between members of the Lodge at their meeting place in what is still today called Sa Maison Gardens at Floriana, and this brought in the Inquisitor to curtail such activities.

Like his predecessor, De Rohan was also awarded the Stock and Pilier by the Pope. Very likely not as much of an encouragement as in recognition of his wise rule. But then how wisely he ruled is reflected in the long lull which the Order and Malta enjoyed during his reign. Apart from what has already been mentioned, the Order had no troubles. Of course barring the common knowledge of its decadence which no one could then stop; and also the always mounting foreboding of how the future political situation in Western Europe would effect it. It had to be an enlightened and courageous De Rohan to go ahead with plans to build the library which Pinto had failed to do. This was no mean task. What was planned was a large-scale architectural master-piece to contain not only the Order's monuments and collections of books, but also its store of bullion. And De Rohan left no stone unturned to make this one of the greatest achievements, as if he knew it was going to be the last construction of its kind to be built by the Order of St John in Malta.

Designed by the Roman architect Stefano Ittar its building began in 1786. It was completed ten years later. Besides the thousands of volumes and other documents transferred from the vestry of St John's Church, the library received one of the richest collections of Groliers and other early bindings, as well as fore-edged paintings. There were also illuminated manuscripts of the thirteenth, fourteenth and fifteenth centuries which came from the Hospitaller Foundation of St Antoine de Viennois with their most coveted treasure being the famous 'Life of St Anthony the Abbot'. There were also two hundred paintings in grisaille by Master Robin Forner of Avignon done in 1426. While the first library was in the vestry of St John's Church it was limited for use by the knights, but now the new one was being built by De Rohan with the condition that its treasures will be made accessible for use by the general public.

It was built in Treasury Square. So called because the spot faced the former Treasury of the Order, now the handsome Casino Maltese, an elite social club. And it could not have been given a better location. Flanked by the grand masters' palace, it was a magnificent monument of the knights then, as it is still today, nearly 200 years later.

* * *

When De Rohan started with the building of the Malta Library he was constrained to turn his attention elsewhere. Until then he had been absorbed in domestic affairs, but now circumstances made it incumbent on him and his knights to grapple with the problems that could arise by the revolution in France that everyone could see approaching.

As a loyal knight and grand master, De Rohan's sympathies were of course for the survival of the Order. But as a Frenchman he also had his loyalties for France represented by her King Louis XVI and his Queen Marie Antoinette. Both of them were personal friends of his. And he was certainly not to be expected to support what views of subversive nature were being put forward at the time. After his election as grand master he had resumed his links with King Louis XVI and sent him a marble cippus, one of a pair discovered in Malta in 1697 bearing inscriptions which placed them amongst the most important epigraphs of antiquity, and contributing conclusive evidence of the decipherment of the Phoenician language. This cippus eventually finished at the Louvre where it is still held as a prize possession. There was also correspondence with Queen Marie-Antoinette, and the Malta Library still holds at least one of her seductive letters to the grand master cajoling him into receiving into the Order the son of a French courtier whose family tree failed to fulfil the requirements.

Now with the rest of the world De Rohan was following the fate of France when she finished on the edge of bankruptcy after the War of American Independence which came to an end in 1783. Six years of expedients then had never enabled her to balance the budget, until the King however well .meaning committed the mistake of convening the states general which was a sort of Parliament that had not met since 1614. Now its members met in Versailles in May 1789, and notwithstanding what hope and goodwill there was behind the meeting, there was a lot of distrust which crept in between those who were seeking a constitutional government for France and the Court Party which was still insisting that the royal power should remain as absolute as before. The result was a riot by the former who on 14 July 1789 stormed the Bastille, and this sparked the French Revolution.

The knights were not directly involved, but after all feudal privileges were abolished the revolutionaries took hold and placed under their control all the Order's rich commanderies in France and Italy which meant that the Order lost its principal and only remaining source of revenue. Some French knights from these commanderies did indeed come to Malta to escape death. But they were thus only adding a financial burden on the Order since they had lost all their property which was confiscated by the Revolutionary Committee, and were indeed poor. It was Britain that came to the rescue of the Order during those times of tension. And De Rohan was offered compensation for the property that was seized, on the one condition however that he would help in the war against France. And indeed notwithstanding the victories of the French Army in Italy which suggested prudence and neutrality to the Order, there were 482 Maltese sailors recruited for the British fleet which was besieging Toulon, while the harbour and dockyard at Malta were offered for use by British Admiral

National Library, Valletta

Hood. The French probably came to know of this interference by the Order. But even before notching it down for future reference, there was a more serious intervention by the grand master.

Moreover with the new and tense situation there was a marked increase in partisan spirit amongst the knights which was characterized by animosity towards the French. In that year, 1790, the Pope's Nuncio at the Maltese Court had occasion to write to the cardinal secretary of state about an official banquet given by Portuguese, Spaniards, Italian and German knights to the exclusion of the French. Eventually, the grand master had good reason to become perturbed by the more frequent duels that were going on between French and Italian knights, even on mere trifles connected with theatrical performances. In one instance the French knights gave vent to their animosity by opposing the arming of a Venetian vessel in harbour. For two nights they stalked the streets of Valletta in search of Venetian officers, and they even went to the Venetian admiral Condulmer asking him to punish his own officers. Instead, the admiral had the French knights arrested, and punished.

The King and Queen of France were menaced, and realising the danger they were in, decided to flee to Varennes and leave the country. Being the upright man he was, and a true friend De Rohan sent them some of his silver plate to help them defray the expenses of their flight since all their money had been confiscated. Only that their well laid plans failed, and both of them were captured and placed under arrest. On learning of this De Rohan was struck by an apoplexy.

Nonetheless he recovered to live another six years. This was unfortunate for him since he had to follow the end of his august friends Louis and Marie Antoinette who were beheaded in January 1793. But then his death in 1797 saved him from having to live through the storm that was to hit the Order after its lull throughout this reign.

During the last year or two of his reign he had not failed to anticipate the end of the Order. It had long been rumoured amongst the knights that the last grand master would be a German. And knowing that his likely successor would be Hompesch, De Rohan prophesied whilst on his death bed that he would be the last grand master to reign in Malta.

*   *   *

The French Revolution spread like wildfire. First all over France, and then elsewhere in Europe when its leaders, exulted as they were in their success, decided to carry the war into the countries of those who did not agree with their doctrines of Liberty, Equality and Fraternity which became the revolution's motto. The revolutionary armies then invaded Belgium, Holland and Germany. Then France also declared war against Britain.

Out of all the turmoil and bloodshed in France one young man rapidly emerged to the fore, Napoleon Bonaparte. Born in Corsica in 1769 he became a lieutenant in the French artillery at a time when the new Republic needed young officers. But although he was still a beginner in the arts of war the young Bonaparte got his chance of a lifetime when in 1795 he helped to crush a serious rising in Paris. From then he never looked back and by 1797 he rose to the rank of general to conduct several successful campaigns in Italy, and was soon being acknowledged as the greatest soldier in France.

With many European countries under his control Napoleon Bonaparte had another of his sensational whims of exploiting the unrest that had arisen in India. He decided to occupy that country and build a great French empire in the east. But first he had to conquer Egypt and use it as a springboard. The only difficulty in his way was Britain which was still outside the group of subject nations. And while France was endowed with the biggest army of the time, the British had the strongest navy, with a substantial fleet in the Mediterranean under Admiral Horatio Nelson. Bonaparte knew he had first to elude the British navy if he were to reach Egypt in such strength as to be able to continue with his plans. And this made him think of using Malta as a stepping stone on his way to Egypt. He knew of the island's strategic position which at that time was her only asset, as he was also aware of Britain's good relations with Malta making the island the last place where the British would think of looking for him. He had always had a bad opinion of the Order which he described as an institution to support in idleness the younger sons of certain privileged families. Then he was on record to have expressed himself to Charles Maurice Talleyrand the

French Minister of External Affairs, as being in favour of capturing Malta, Cyprus and Gibraltar, in that order, to get a strong hold on the Mediterranean.

Following De Rohan's death in 1798, the knights of Malta had elected for the first time and as had been constantly rumoured, a German grand master, Ferdinand von Hompesch. None denies that he was kind, good-natured and affable. But then there were many who also claimed that he was feeble and indecisive. This poses the question as to why then he was chosen as grand master at a time when the future of the Order was already being seen as having to depend on him? Could this have been a ruse of the French knights who had already begun speaking freely and betraying their wishes not to have to resist the new fraternity of progress? The fact that they chose a German as they said they would do and not one of their own also makes food for thought.

Whatever it was, Hompesch did not have much time on his hands to do what other grand masters had done. Because he was the kind of person he was, and the only grand master who could speak Maltese, he immediately became popular, and he furthered this by giving his patronage to several localities, erecting an arch or some other feature in his commemoration. But that was all he could do. As for larger works he had neither the money nor the time. This he spent in looking at Europe. Not for money, moral or political support as the Order had always done, but to follow Napoleon's movements and try to find out whether Malta featured in his plans. But even so, very little of Napoleon's rumblings seem to have affected him. For he is reported to have been an optimist who overlooked all military preparations and laughed at what forebodings there were made by old knights whom he called alarmists; and maintaining that all his knights were loyal. Even when it was pointed out to him that whilst he chose to go about in his ceremonial clothes, de Valette used to be more often seen with the armour and helmet, he was left unruffled.

As was to be proved by history Hompesch was wrong because unknown to him he was surrounded by traitors. Many of these belonged to the Revolutionary Club that was set in Malta with its members meeting at the house of the secretary of the Order's Treasurer Bosredon de Ransipt at the village of Lija. There were amongst them Deodat de Dolomiere and Prince Camille de Rohan, the nephew of the previous grand master both of whom had become ardent followers of the Revolution.

Hompesch could have taken a hint from the arrest of Pierre Francois Louis Doublet a humble donat of the Order, who it was alleged, had sold the magisterial cipher of the Order to the enemy. There were many other members of the Order who seem to have been supporters of the French revolutionary army. Besides that, there were also Maltese who supported the French, one of these being Mikiel Anton Vassalli, known as the father of Maltese language.

There was also Poussielgue, a French who used to visit Malta very often saying he came to see his cousin, the captain of the Port, and spent his time disseminating information about the Revolution. He must have deluded many of the young knights as well as some of the older ones, making them ask themselves whether their life in poverty and exile in the Order has been worthwhile.

One wonders then how Hompesch could have remained cool and impervious when a dozen or so of his French knights suddenly left the Convent to join the Revolutionaries, or better still as some have interpreted it, to leave the sinking ship.

The French general had been building an armada at Toulon, Marseilles and Genoa leaving everyone to guess his intentions. Including Admiral Nelson whose string of victories and long endeavours at sea stretched as long as were Napoleon's campaigns on land. Now the British admiral was scouring the Mediterranean trying to intercept the French when they left harbour.

It was on 8 May, 1798 that Napoleon set out with his armada. It was a force made up of thirteen sail-of-the-line, eight frigates plus two Venetian 64 gunships, with six other frigates and other small craft; seventy two naval ships in all. But then there were 400 transports carrying some 36,000 troops. As it was, Nelson got to know that the French were on the move, and either making a bad guess or because of false information he received, he went to look for the armada in the Eastern Mediterranean. But Napoleon was heading for Malta, and in the afternoon on 9 June 1798 he had his first look at the impressive battlements of the island which was to be his first prey.

The lookouts on Malta's bastions and soon after also the knights saw the 472 sails. It was a terrifying sight, and never since the time of de Valette had such a large enemy force come so close to the island. With the big difference of course that while in 1565 the Order had been waiting and prepared for the attack, now in contrast there were the unmanned fortifications as Hompesch had been caught by surprise. But even if he had taken the previous warnings it would not have made any difference because the knights had neither the men nor armaments to resist such force.

A French pinnace soon brought a request from Napoleon to the grand master asking for permission to enter harbour and take on water. However weak, Hompesch was not that stupid, and after consulting his council replied, quoting the Treaty of Utrecht that with Malta being a neutral port he could only allow four belligerent ships to enter harbour at a time. This was the kind of reply Napoleon wanted, and after exercising the tyrant's gambit of flying into a rage when frustrated, he shouted: 'Water is refused, so we will go to take it.' And that was that.

Even if Hompesch had the men and will to resist, as some still feel he should have done, it would still have been impossible for him to do it. Because as has been mentioned some spies and troublemakers had already been put ashore who had established contact with the French knights. Collaboration was then also assured from the officer commanding the artillery on the fortifications as well as from the Order's senior engineer Toussand. All the fortifications were manned, although the officers were not helping out that much. There were officers who were openly in favour of the French and were seen helping in the destabilising atmosphere of the moment. There were others who were well organised and offered a lot of resistance. The French landed in four different locations, making a much organised landing and attack. Although there was enthusiasm in the defence of certain parts of the island, the defenders were outnumbered, outmanoeuvred and not well supplied with ammunition. In Gozo there was also some resistance, although the officers soon surrendered. But by darkness all defence crumbled in front of the French Grenadiers who had penetrated everywhere. As if not to be left out, three ships of the Order returning laden with booty from an action against Algiers, sailed into the French fleet off Malta to be obviously seized. Two of them, the *San Giovanni* and *San Zaccaria* were immediately put into service by the French who changed their names to Dego and Beruse.

That night the Maltese islands became a French possession. On 11 June then, the knights agreed to the surrender terms, and thus signed away every vestige of the sovereignty they had over Malta which thus passed out of their hands after 268 years of rule.

The French troops landing at Malta, 9 June 1798

18

THE AFTERMATH

The Order's downfall in Malta had a stunning effect. The faithful knights had never expected this kind of outcome. And they could only follow in stupefied silence as Napoleon Bonaparte issued his specific instructions in their regard. Grand Master Hompesch was to retain his military honours and receive a golden handshake of an annual pension of 300,000 francs. But then he and such of the knights that could prove to be dangerous were given three days to leave Malta with their private property. When asked if they could take with them the relic of the hand of the Baptist, Bonaparte contemptuously replied: 'They may keep the dead hand, but the ring on the finger looks better on mine.' Then he slipped off the bejewelled ring from the relic and placed it on his finger.

Hompesch then made his way with some of the knights to Trieste, but the rest made their way to St Petersburg in Russia seeking the protection of Emperor Paul, also offering him the dignity of grand master that had been vacated by Hompesch. This proclamation of a married non-Catholic as a head of the Order was wholly illegal and void, as it was indeed never recognised by the Holy See. What old knights remained in Malta because of their inability to travel were to be given a pension of 1,000 livres if they were over sixty, and 700 livres to those who were younger.

A symbolic end to the Order's naval history might have been reflected in the death of its last admiral Francesco Caracciolo at the hands of Nelson. The Neopolitan admiral who had become the Order's captain general of the galleys in 1795, who was indeed a friend of the British commander-in-chief, was allowed to take service under the Parthenopian Republic after Malta's collapse. But soon after this Republic's fall, he was given a safe conduct to cross again to the British side. Only that such genuine movements seem to have been misinterpreted by Nelson who allowed his friend to be arrested and venially court-martialed which led to him being hung at the yardarm of his own ship Minerva at Naples on 29 June 1799.

The Maltese people were stunned into submission by the French occupation. They had never expected it to come so fast and in the way it did. It is true that as a gesture of goodwill Bonaparte released Don Gaetan Mannarino from prison after he had been put there by Ximenes. But then after setting up his headquarters at Parisio Palace in Valletta (today housing the Ministry of Foreign Affairs) he began with his zest for organisation to turn Malta into an orderly department of the French Republic. Even this did not worry the Maltese unduly. The worst came when the French began a systematic plundering of churches and private property. There was soon collected a storehouse of gold, silver and precious stones, as well as paintings and other priceless items. The bulk of the silver from the Order's hospital and Sacra Infirmeria was melted to make 3,500 lbs. of bullion which was to be used for paying French troops on the Egyptian campaign. All this booty was then loaded in the general's flagship *L'Orient* that was leading the armada in which there were now also being pressed Maltese lads as soldiers and sailors, against their will.

Bonaparte left Malta after six days, leaving behind him 3,053 infantrymen as well as three companies of artillery under General Vaubois to garrison the island. It would not come as a surprise if the Maltese now began to see the departed knights in a new light, realizing no doubt that they would have preferred the devil they knew than the one they didn't know. Even so they were not taking the French occupation lying down. Their fervour for freedom and democracy generated the seed of revolt and three months later they rose against the French. This time there were no half measures as in the uprising against Ximenes. But people from all walks of life including priests and professionals took part and the French forces were soon cleared from the countryside and shut up in Valletta, Vittoriosa and Senglea. It was two years later, in September 1800 that with the help of the British, the French forces were evicted from Malta completely.

There followed a period of flux and uncertainty for Malta when hard-pressed by poverty and disease the inhabitants were hoping to consolidate their newly found freedom by asking Britain to take Malta under her protection and obviate another attack by the French. Britain agreed to do this for the duration of her still raging war with France, and Captain Alexander Ball RN was appointed as the first civil commissioner. But even so, there was a problem in that by right Malta still belonged to the Kingdom of the Two Sicilies. And with this power being unable to take over, there was the grand priory of Russia created in 1797 with Czar Paul as grand master of the Sovereign Order who was contending for the island. For a time it seemed as if the knights would after all return to Malta. However there was now resentment from the Maltese. They knew how their forefathers had been treated by the knights, and taking the good and the bad into consideration they had drawn out a balance sheet of their feelings which left them determined not to be involved again with the Order of St John.

Still, the situation had turned into one where the Maltese and their feelings did not count. And this because of a change of government in Britain with the new administration wanting peace with France at all costs which led to the Peace Treaty of Amiens on 27 March 1802. And included in this treaty there was the placing of Malta under the dominion of the knights of St John, with the provision of a garrison by His Sicilian Majesty, and the guarantees of Prussia, Russia and Austria. So it seemed to be destined to have the knights back in Malta, even if at that time the Order had been impoverished further after having been just despoiled by Bonaparte of its revenues in Piedmont and Parma in Italy. But none lost sight of the fact that failing this it would be tantamount to handing Malta back to Bonaparte and France. And this was pressed home even as the first Neopolitan troops arrived in Malta on 8 October 1802 in compliance with one of the conditions in the treaty.

Concurrently with this part of history in the making there was unexpected support from the British press and people with various attacks on the government for letting Malta go again to the Order, and ultimately to France. British public opinion was all in favour of retaining the island, and this had the desired effect. On 17 October 1802 the British secretary of state for the Colonies gave secret instructions to Sir Alexander Ball in Malta to suspend all measures for evacuating Malta.

This new British attitude must have become evident to all the other parties concerned, for there was soon the Pope hastening the process by selecting Chevalier Ruspoli as the new grand master for Malta in succession to the assassinated Czar Paul. And when Ruspoli refused, there was the immediate appointment of Bailiff Giovanni Tommasi instead, who was sent to Messina in Sicily to await the word to cross over to Malta. But Alexander Ball was quick to advise the grand master not to go, as the Maltese were hostile to him. To the plenipotentiary then who went to him and asked for the early evacuation of British troops from Malta, Ball merely said that he had still to await instructions. These were of course delaying tactics as Britain by now had no intention of abandoning Malta. Bonaparte however was not deluded and he came out into the open and showed to one and all that it was him who had all the time been pulling 'the strings. Now he delivered an ultimatum to Britain. She was to surrender Malta, or he would again declare war on her. And Britain replied, choosing war, which the French then declared on 16 May 1803.

There were then to be no further attempts for a comeback by the Order which went into temporary retirement, and this ironically enough being characterised by the death of the discredited and forgotten Hompesch at Montpellier where he was living as a destitute and lonely exile not having enough money even for his funeral. A month later the last Grand Master Tommasi died as well. Malta continued to have the protection of Britain throughout her war with France which eventually came to an end after Bonaparte by now Emperor of France was defeated in 1814. This was an end characterised by two important events – the abdication of Bonaparte and his transfer to the island of Elba, and – the Treaty of Paris on 30 May 1814 laying down amongst other things, that the Island of Malta and its Dependencies were to belong in full right and sovereignty of His Britannic Majesty. It was the end of an era and the preface to a

Captain Alexander Ball

history with Malta as a British Colony. But that is another story.

It was in 1805 that the Order set out on its revival. Operating from temporary seats in Messina, Catania and Ferrara, the number of knights that rallied to the clarion call did not justify the appointment of a grand master. So, for the first time, the leadership was entrusted to a lieutenant-master, with the first one to be elected being Fra Innico-Maria Guevara Suardo. He reigned until 1814, just enough to see the abdication of Napoleon Bonaparte, but also to perceive the dying out of what still glowing embers remained of the Order's desire to return to Malta, when the island became a British colony. And this must have now dimmed any hopes the Order might have had for the future.

But Bonaparte stoked again the fires of history when after

The surrender of the French forces from Malta by the British, 4 September 1800

escaping from Elba in 1815, he reappeared to be finally defeated at the battle of Waterloo on 18 June of that same year. Now he was transferred to the island of St Helena, allowing Europe to breathe freely again .and to continue with the restoration of kings and the old order. There was now also the Papal Bull issued in 1814 to make the Order look ahead, and indeed the various Langues that had been subdued during the turmoil that had just ended now began to take life again. Only that the Langues of Aragon, Castile and Portugal were annexed to their national sovereigns, while Italy was not yet a nation. The German and Anglo-Bavarian Langues had dispersed beyond revival, and the Order had to look elsewhere for a comeback.

In the meantime Andre di Giovanni had succeeded Suardo as lieutenant-master, but although he reigned until 1821, the wanted opportunity eluded him. It was during the reign of his successor Antoine Busca that there was revived the Langue of England in 1827. But again the Order was faced with problems when the Langue opted to admit Protestants into its ranks, which was something that went against the statute of the Sovereign Order. It was this in fact that made the revived Langues turn into a different body called the Venerable Langue, with the Reverend Sir Robert Peat being elected as its grand prior on 29 January 1831.

Strangely enough the new Venerable Langue continued to function as if it was still an integral part of the Sovereign and Catholic Order of Malta. Even to the extent of acknowledging its superior Anton Fusca, and Charles Candida who succeeded him in 1834, as well as the Pope who was the Order's spiritual head. But none could deny that all this was most irregular. The more so that by now the Order had already had its first knight, Nonious Alvares Pereira canonised and declared Blessed by Pope Benedict XV, as there were indeed others to follow. Matters finally came to a head in 1858 when the Venerable Langue splintered from the Sovereign Order of Malta and declared its own sovereignty under the new title of the Sovereign and Illustrious Order of St John of Jerusalem which later was to become known as the Venerable Order of St John of Jerusalem, with its most important achievement being the subsequent organisation of the St John Ambulance Brigade, still functioning to these very days.

There was still what could be called further splintering when after old Langues were disbanded, new National Knights Associations were founded. As there were also to be some independent Orders to be established in England, Germany, Sweden, Holland and also in the United States and Canada. All of these bearing the name of St John and wearing as their insignia the white eight-pointed cross. Some of these orders consisted mostly of non-Catholic members who linked their tradition to the old Priories of the Sovereign Order of Jerusalem which were suppressed or transformed in those countries at the time of the Reformation. The rest were bogus organisations with no connection to the real Order of St John, except in name and dress.

Nothing of this affected the Sovereign Military Order of Malta which continued with the strict selection of its members who were henceforth not to be called for any military duty, since such a requirement had been abolished. There was also established the new principle of sovereignty without territorial possessions, except those of the Malta palace at 68 Via Condotti in Rome which was also established as the Order's seat in 1834, and the Villa on the Aventine, also in Rome. But the Order continued and even increased its hospitaller work, and this soon led to the restoration of its old dignity, under the Pontificate of Leo XIII in 1879. Now the Order had its seventy fourth grand master, Giovanni Battista Ceschi a Santa Croce who also re-established the association of the Italian Langue. In the old tradition Ceschi was also made a prince and as such had the right to all sovereign honours. But the most important fact was that the Order could now send and receive diplomatic envoys, and this was duly recognised by all Catholic heads of state. It was thus that the Sovereign and Military Order of Malta came back on its feet.

Throughout the years that followed then, and right into the twentieth century its name and fame expanded worldwide through its hospitaller and welfare work. Its hospitals began to sprout up, and today besides in Italy these can be found in the leper colonies in Africa and also in China. Its humane activities during World War I were considerable while it continued with its good work during World War II under Grand Master Ludovico Chigi della Rovere Albani, when it also rendered sterling service in compliance with the Geneva Convention, and this of course without discriminating between races, colour and sides. Its good work continued in the post war period right to our times, and this comprised the establishment of a Blood Bank in Malta.

Today the Sovereign Military Order of Malta under Grand Master Fra Matthew Festing is spread world-wide. It maintains diplomatic relations through accredited representatives with the Holy See, nine European nations, nineteen states in South America, three in Asia, and twenty three in Africa. Moreover it maintains delegations in the Council of Europe, in several United Nations Specialized Agencies, and other International Organisations in Geneva. The latest significant move in this regard came in 1991 when the Order took up the commitment to restore parts of Fort St Angelo in Malta with the scope of having the fort used in future as a residence for novices and dignitaries of the Order, as well as visiting guests. Could this move be considered as a symbolic return of the order to Malta which would be an achievement worthy to rank in its thousand years of history? After all it is in Malta that the raison d'etre it had always shed throughout its centuries of existence can still be found.

For throughout the island, the magnificent fortifications, the churches, auberges and other palatial − buildings that were built during its 268 year stay still stand; hallowed by time and history. It's more like an aura that can still be recognised in the Maltese people's customs, language and culture. As it can also be traced in their names and ways of living. Then, notwithstanding the five centuries that have almost passed, which include a 180 year British occupation, and a devastating war which required an extensive rebuilding programme, going along the narrow streets of the island dwarfed by buildings that still bear the patina of their time, one cannot fail to sense still the strong presence of the knights of Malta.

THE GRAND MASTERS OF MALTA
AND THEIR
COAT OF ARMS

Phillipe Villiers de
L'Isle-Adam

1521   1534

Pietro del Ponte

1534   1535

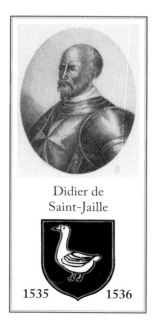

Didier de
Saint-Jaille

1535   1536

Juan de Homedes

1536   1553

Claude de la Sengle

1553   1557

Jean de Valette

1557 1568

Pietro del Monte

1568 1572

Jean L'Eveque
de la Cassiere

1572 1581

Hugues Loubenx
de Verdalle

1582 1595

Martin Garzes

1595 1601

Alof de Wignacourt

1601 1622

Luis Mendez
de Vasconcellos

1622   1623

Antoine de Paule

1623   1636

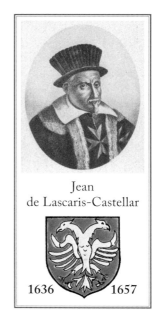

Jean
de Lascaris-Castellar

1636   1657

Martin de Redin

1657   1660

Annet
de Clermont-Gessan

1660

Raphael Cotoner

1660   1663

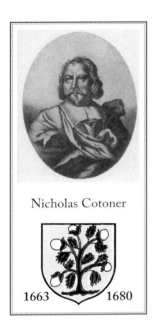

Nicholas Cotoner

1663   1680

Gregorio Carafa

1680   1690

Adrien de Wignacourt

1690   1697

Raymond Perellos
y Roccaful

1697   1720

Marc' Antonio
Zondadari

1720   1722

Antonio Manoel
de Vilhena

1722   1736

Ramon Despuig

1736 1741

Manoel Pinto
de Fonseca

1741 1773

Francesco Ximenes
de Texada

1773 1775

Emmanuel
de Rohan-Polduc

1775 1797

Ferdinand
von Hompesch

1797 1799

THE EIGHT LANGUES
OF THE ORDER

Langue of Italy

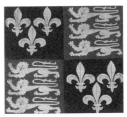

Langue of England

Langue of Auvergne

Langue of Germany

Langue of Provence

Langue of France

Langue of Castile

*Langue of Aragon
and Navarre*

GRAND MASTERS OF THE ORDER

IN PALESTINE

The Blessed Gerard . . . . 1099 — 1120
Blessed Raymond du Puy. . . . . 1120 — 1160
Auger de Balben . . . . 1160 — 1162
Arnaud de Comps. . . . . 1162 — 1163
Gilbert d'Aissailly . . . . 1163 — 1170
Gastone de Murols . . . . 1170 — 1172
Jobert de Syria . . . . 1172 — 1177
Roger de Moulins . . . . 1177 — 1187
Armengol de Aspa . . . . 1187 — 1190
Garnier de Naplous . . . . 1190 — 1192
Geoffroy de Donjon. . . . . 1193 — 1202
Alphonse de Portugal. . . . . 1202 — 1206
Geoffrod le Rat . . . . 1206 — 1207
Garin de Montaigu . . . . 1207 — 1228
Bertrand de Thessy . . . . 1228 — 1231
Guerin de Montacute. . . . . 1231 — 1236
Bertrand de Comps . . . . 1236 — 1240
Pierre de Vielle Bride . . . . 1240 — 1242
Guillaume de Chateauneuf. . . . . 1242 — 1258
Hugues Revel . . . . 1258 — 1277
Nicolas Lorgne . . . . 1277 — 1284
Jean de Villiers . . . . 1284 — 1288

IN CYPRUS

Jean de Villiers . . . . 1289 — 1294
Odon des Pins . . . . 1294 — 1296
Guillaume de Villaret . . . . 1296 — 1305
Foulques de Villaret . . . . 1305 — 1308

IN RHODES

Foulques de Villaret . . . . 1308 — 1319
Helion de Villeneuve . . . . 1319 — 1346
Dieudonné de Gozon . . . . 1346 — 1353
Pierre de Corneillan . . . . 1353 — 1355
Roger de Pins . . . . 1355 — 1365
Raymond Berengar . . . . 1365 — 1374
Robert de Juliac . . . . 1374 — 1376
Jean Fernandez de Heredia . . . . 1376 — 1396
Riccardo Caracciolo *(rival grand master)* . . . . . 1383 — 1395
Philibert de Naillac . . . . 1396 — 1421
Antoine Fluvian de la Rivière . . . . 1421 — 1437
Jean de Lastic . . . . 1437 — 1454
Jacques de Milly . . . . 1454 — 1461
Pere Raymond Sacosta . . . . 1461 — 1467
Jean Baptist Orsini . . . . 1467 — 1476
Pierre d'Aubusson . . . . 1476 — 1503
Emery d'Amboise . . . . 1503 — 1512
Guy de Blanchefort . . . . 1512 — 1513
Fabrizio del Carretto . . . . 1513 — 1521
Philippe Villiers de L'Isle-Adam . . . . 1521 — 1530

IN MALTA

Philippe Villiers de L'Isle-Adam . . . . 1530 — 1534
Pietro del Ponte . . . . 1534 — 1535
Didier de Saint-Jaille . . . . 1535 — 1536
Juan de Homedes . . . . 1536 — 1553
Claude de la Sengle . . . . 1553 — 1557
Jean Parisot de la Valette . . . . 1557 — 1568
Pietro del Monte . . . . 1568 — 1572
Jean l'Eveque de la Cassiere . . . . 1572 — 1581
Hugues Loubenx de Verdalle . . . . 1582 — 1595
Martin Garzes . . . . 1595 — 1601
Alof de Wignacourt . . . . 1601 — 1622
Luis Mendez de Vasconcellos . . . . 1622 — 1623
Antoine de Paule . . . . 1623 — 1636
Jean de Lascaris-Castellar . . . . 1636 — 1657
Martin de Redin . . . . 1657 — 1660
Annet de Clermont-Gessan 1660
Raphael Cotoner . . . . 1660 — 1663
Nicolas Cotoner . . . . 1663 — 1680
Gregorio Carafa . . . . 1680 — 1690
Adrien de Wignacourt . . . . 1690 — 1697

Ramon Perellos y Roccaful	1697 — 1720
Marc' Antonio Zondadari	1720 — 1722
Antonio Manoel de Vilhena	1722 — 1736
Ramon Despuig	1736 — 1741
Manoel Pinto de Fonseca	1741 — 1773
Francisco Ximenes de Texada	1773 — 1775
Emmanuel de Rohan-Polduc	1775 — 1797
Ferdinand von Hompesch	1797 — 1799

IN RUSSIA

Paul I, Emperor of Russia	1798 — 1801

IN SICILY

Giovanni Battista Tommasi	1803 — 1805

IN ITALY

Giovanni Battista Ceschi a Santa Croce	1879 — 1905
Galeazzo von Thun und Hohenstein	1905 — 1931
Ludovico Chigi Albani della Rovere	1931 — 1951
Angelo de Mojana di Cologna	1962 — 1988
Andrew Bertie	1988 — 2008
Matthew Festing	2008 —

LIEUTENANT GRANDMASTERS

Count Nikolay Saltykov	1801 — 1803
Innico Maria Guevara-Suardo	1805 — 1814
André di Giovanni	1814 — 1821
Antoine Busca	1821 — 1834
Carlo Candida	1834 — 1845
Philippe di Colloredo-Mels	1845 — 1864
Alessandro Borgia	1865 — 1871
Giovanni Battista Ceschi a Santa Croce	1871 — 1879
Pie Franchi de Cavalieri	1929 — 1931
(appointed to stand in for the indisposed grand master at the time)	
Antonio Hercolani-Fava-Simonetti	1951 — 1955
Ernesto Paternó Castello di Carcaci	1955 — 1962
Jean Charles Pallavicini	1988
Giacomo dalla Torre del Tempio di Sanguinetto	2008

BIBLIOGRAPHY

Anonymous, *Nouvelle relation du voyage et description exacte de L'Isle de Malte* (Paris,1679)

Azzopardi, Rev.John (Editor), *The Church of St John in Valletta* (Malta, 1978)

Bradford, Ernle, *The Great Siege* (London, 1961)

Brockman, Eric, *Last Bastion* (London, 1961)

Brydone, Patrick, *A Tour through Sicily and Malta* (London, 1773)

Curry, E. Hamilton, *Seawolves of the Mediterranean* (London, 1908)

Fugger Newsletter, (London, 1924)

Galea, Michael, *The German Knights in Malta* (Malta, 1986)

Hardman, J., *History of Malta during the French and British occupations*, 1798-1815 (London, 1909)

Laspina, Rev. S., *Outlines of Maltese History* (Malta, 1947)

Luke, Sir Harry, *Malta – An Account and an Appreciation* (London, 1949)

Mackenzie-Grieve, Averil, *A Knight of St John* (Unpublished)

Mifsud, Alfred, *Knights Hospitallers of the Venerable tongue of England in Malta* (New York, 1914)

Plaisse, Andre, *Le Rouge de Malte* (Rennes, 1991)

Prokowoski, Rudolph, *The Order of St John* (Vatican City, 1950)

Rayner, Robert M., *Concise History of Britain* (London, 1946)

Schermerhorn, Elizabeth, *Malta of the Knights* (London, 1929)

Serenata, 1760, *Le Balliche Contingenze d'Europa*

Spreti, Marchese Camillo, *The Manuscript of a Knight of Malta* (As edited by Averil Mackenzie-Grieve)

Teonge, Rev. Henry, *Diary*

Thomson, George Malcolm, *Sir Francis Drake* (London, 1972)

Vella, Prof. A.P., *The Tribunal of the Inquisition* (Malta, 1964)

Vertot, Abbe de, *History of the knights of Malta* (London, 1729)

LIST OF ILLUSTRATIONS

INDEX

Further suggested reading – www.bdlbooks.com

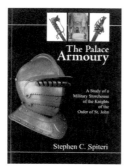

The Palace Armoury
Stephen C. Spiteri

German Knights of Malta
Michael Galea

Fortresses of the Knights
Stephen C. Spiteri

The 1565 Great Siege of
Malta and Hipólito Sans's
La Maltea
Arnold Cassola

Toni Bajada
The Maltese Messenger of
the Grand Master
Emilio Lombardi

The Art of
Fortress Building in
Hospitaller Malta
Stephen C. Spiteri

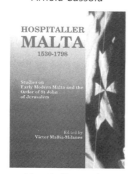

Hospitaller Malta
1530–1798
Victor Mallia-Milanes (ed.)

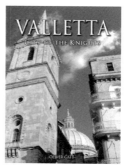

VALLETTA
City of the Knights
Oliver Gatt

The Achievements of
The Knights of Malta
Alexander Sutherland

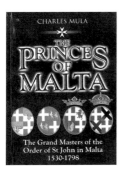

The Princes of Malta
Charles Mula

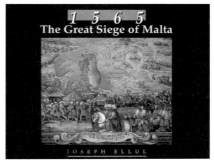

1565 – The Great Siege of Malta
Joseph Ellul

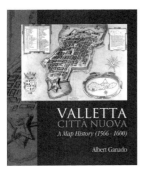

Valletta Città Nuova
A Map History (1566–1600)
Albert Ganado

The Grandmaster's Palace
& the Goblin Tapestries
Joseph Ellul

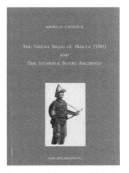

The Great Siege of Malta
(1565) and the Istanbul
State Archives
Arnold Cassola

The Commerce of Oranges
in the XVIIIth Century
Alain Blondy

The Order of Malta
Exposed
Carasi

The First Siege 1565
Victor Pulis